THE COMPLETE BOOK of
CLEAN

TIPS & TECHNIQUES for YOUR HOME

THE COMPLETE BOOK of
CLEAN

TIPS & TECHNIQUES *for* YOUR HOME

by Toni Hammersley

weldon**owen**

Table of Contents

Table of Contents

Table of Contents

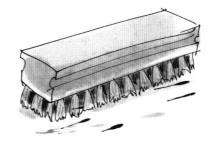

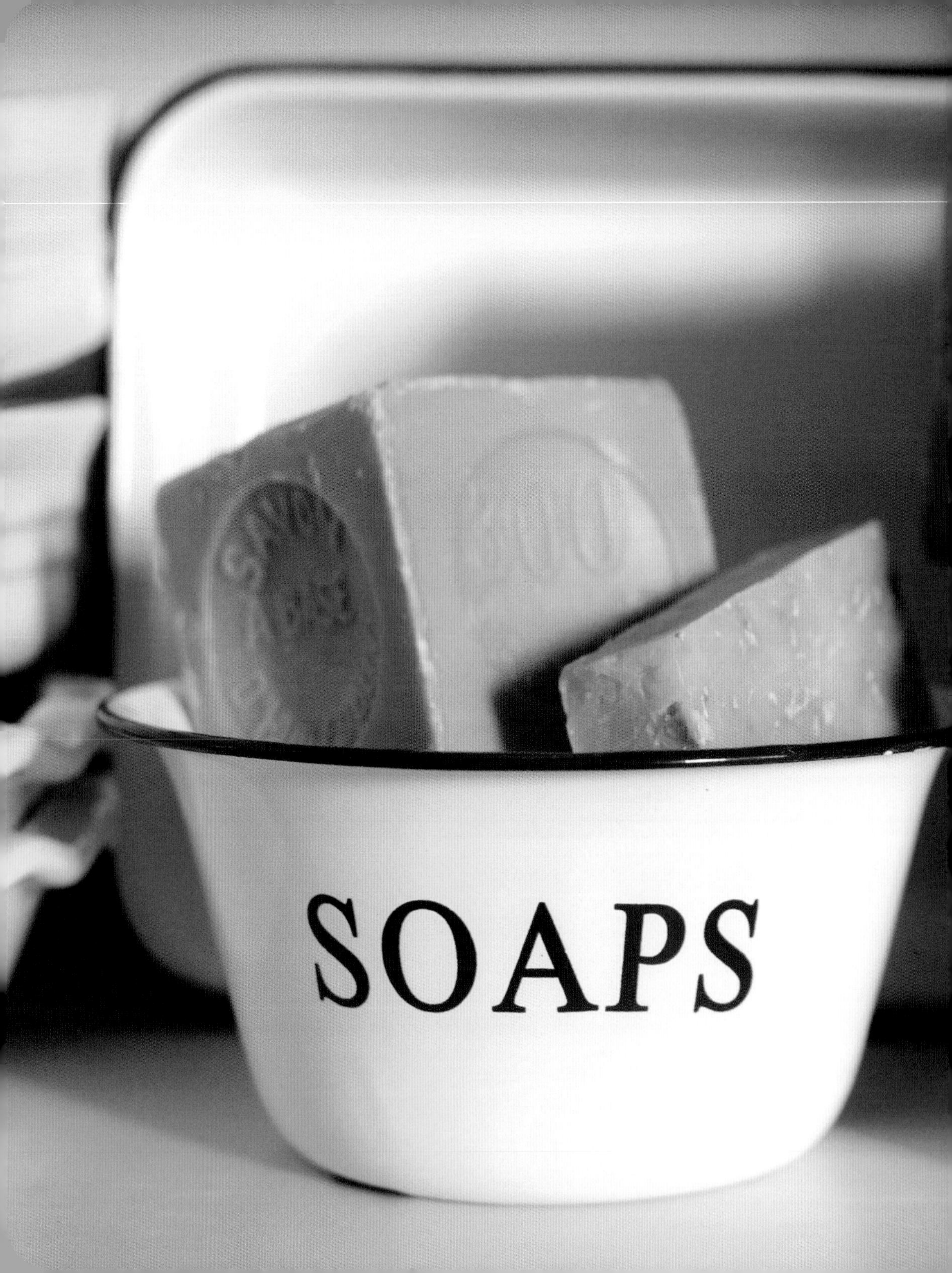
SOAPS

Every day, I find myself sweeping the floors, wiping up spills, picking up clutter, and straightening pillows on the sofa. An hour later, I do it all over again. Messes are a part of life, and cleaning them up is essential to our well-being. Whether you live in a 4,000-square-foot home or a small one-bedroom apartment, implementing a cleaning routine is the key to success.

In this book, you'll find homemade natural cleaning recipes and learn how to put together a green cleaning caddy. You'll also learn my secrets to keeping up with daily, weekly, and monthly chores. I'll share fundamental cleaning checklists, including plans for seasonal home maintenance and detailed spring and fall cleaning. You'll find a multitude of cleaning strategies for the tough jobs and simple tips for the small ones.

We all face challenges when it comes to keeping our homes clean and tidy. You may not have enough time in the day or the energy to keep up, or you're simply overwhelmed. That's normal, and it's OK to feel that way. By taking it one step at a time, you will learn how to conquer the messes and implement a cleaning plan that works for you. As you clean, think about decluttering as well—an organized house is much easier to keep clean. Check out my 30-Bag Purge Challenge at the back of this book for one fun and easy way to cut the clutter.

Give new life to your home and give it the attention it needs. By the time you get to the end of this book, your home will be sparkling clean and you will finally get to enjoy a much-needed Saturday afternoon at the spa. You deserve it! So put on your cleaning gloves, and let's get busy.

Hugs,
Toni

Getting Started

Motivation is the main challenge of a clean home. To help me get (and stay) motivated, I put on comfortable clothes, turn on my favorite music (really loud), and fill the diffuser with my favorite essential oils. And I always start with the big picture in mind. What do you want your home to look like when you're finished? You can accomplish it, one step at a time. My first step is to assemble a cleaning caddy and gather all of the supplies needed to conquer the messes. You'll create several homemade cleaning solutions to get the job done. Then we will concentrate on the chores common to all rooms of the house. I will outline these tasks and offer checklists needed to complete them. Working through the common tasks quickly gives you momentum to keep going. By using a kitchen timer, you can set your pace (and goal) to work efficiently. Let's get started.

001 STOCK YOUR CADDY

Streamline housekeeping duties by assembling a cleaning caddy to contain all necessary supplies needed to keep your home clean. A caddy eliminates time-draining, procrastinating searches for the right supplies and means fewer trips to the store or utility closet. Assemble supplies in a bucket or container with a handle, and everything will be within arm's reach when you need it. Here's a checklist of my suggestions for essential caddy tools.

- ☐ Microfiber cloths
- ☐ Sponge
- ☐ Disposable wipes
- ☐ Duster
- ☐ Lint roller
- ☐ Toothbrush
- ☐ Scrub brush
- ☐ Grout brush
- ☐ Gloves
- ☐ Trash bags
- ☐ Cleaning solutions

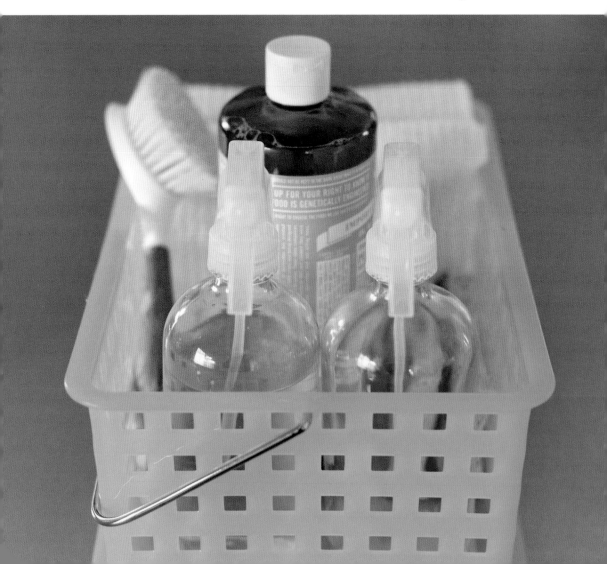

002 WIPE IT ALL UP

You'll want some options for wiping, dusting, and otherwise cleaning various surfaces.

MICROFIBER CLOTHS These soft, multipurpose cloths contribute to a healthier house. Woven from millions of very fine fibers, they snag dirt and bacteria in their web and sweep it away. Even dry or with a small amount of water, they are superior to paper towels or cotton rags when it comes to collecting dust and dirt. Because they absorb grime, clean them after each use by running them through the washing machine. Don't use fabric softener in the dryer with them—it clogs the fibers, reducing their ability to grab dirt.

THE CLASSIC SPONGE A sponge is an essential tool for absorbing spills and washing dishes or counters. Look for nonabrasive types that won't scratch the surface you're cleaning. After each use, clean and sanitize the sponge through a full cycle in the dishwasher or kill the germs in the microwave for two minutes. Be sure the sponge is wet.

DISPOSABLE WIPES Although I advocate reducing, reusing, and recycling as much as possible, there are times when it's necessary to use disposable products like cleaning wipes. Pet accidents and on-the-go messes are great examples. Simply wipe up the mess with a disposable wipe and toss it in the trash.

A DUSTER Microfiber or feather dusters on an extension wand are invaluable in hard-to-reach spaces—think ceiling fans, top shelves, corners, or under the bed.

003 ROLL THAT LINT

A lint brush is a multipurpose tool that is often forgotten among all the cleaning supplies in the caddy. It removes lint from not only clothing but also handbag interiors, lampshades, curtains, furniture, car seats, and flooring. And if you have pets, it's great for animal fur. Now get rolling!

004 DON THE GLOVES

Just like what Grandma used, cleaning gloves keep hands soft and fingernails strong as well as provide a better grip in soapy water. Leave a second pair in a different color in the bathroom for cleaning the toilet.

005 BRUSH IT OFF

My three favorite brushes for cleaning are a toothbrush, a scrub brush, and a grout brush. Each has its unique properties, so use them all accordingly.

TOOTHBRUSH A handy implement for dirty surfaces in the bathroom and kitchen, a toothbrush allows you to scrub messes and stains on a small scale.

SCRUB BRUSH A natural wooden bristle brush is a tried-and-true tool that cleans just about everything from pots and pans to outdoor furniture. When it's time to clean a wooden brush, douse it in warm, soapy water and remove stubborn dirt with an old toothbrush. Air-dry it with bristles facing down so water will drain from the wood and minimize the chances that it will warp or grow mildew.

GROUT BRUSH For those hard-to-clean stains, a brush that's designed specifically for grout is needed to lift dirt and grime. A grout brush is equipped with particularly stiff V-shaped bristles that can get into the grout lines easier, and does an overall better job than other types of brushes.

006 BAG YOUR TRASH

Keep several large and small trash bags in the cleaning caddy to make chore days go smoother. Why run up and down the stairs several times to get more bags? Keep it simple and stock the caddy well!

Spring CLEANING BOX

Blogger Nikki Boyd has created a very helpful tool for anyone getting ready to do an annual Spring Cleaning—whether you're just setting up a routine or looking to fine-tune one you've been been using for years. Get the whole family involved and turn cleaning into a fun activity for all.

NIKKI BOYD, *AT HOME WITH NIKKI*

My Spring Cleaning Box is a tool I have used for years to help complete my annual home-cleaning project. It truly makes the task of spring cleaning a simple process—I don't have to reinvent the wheel each year, and I can simply add, eliminate, or modify cards whenever I redecorate.

HOW IT WORKS The Spring Cleaning Box is filled with index cards that identify all the tasks I tackle each year to keep my home sparkling. It's categorized by each room, and within each category is a card for each task that needs to be accomplished in that room.

I keep the box on our entryway table, and each member of my family chooses a few cards each day during the spring-cleaning month. The family goal is to complete the tasks on their cards by the end of the day. As we complete each task, we place the card in the "Completed" section of the box. Seeing that section grow over time provides a great sense of accomplishment—as does seeing the number of remaining tasks disappear!

TO ASSEMBLE To make the cards, I simply use cardstock, write specific tasks on each card, and laminate them for durability. If you have small children, you may want to use a different color for cards labeled with kid-friendly tasks. You can use a recipe box, one designed for business cards, or any container that fits your cards.

Once your box is stocked and ready to go, the only thing left is to get your family on board. Remember: You want to make it fun! Offer a prize to the family member who completes the most cards, or come up with a special treat that everyone can enjoy.

The Spring Cleaning Box transforms a mundane task into a game and makes the cleaning process a team effort. It's become a tradition in at my house, and my family knows it's spring-cleaning season when they see the teal box!

Nikki Boyd is a talented home organizing and decorating blogger. Her tips can be found at www.athomewithnikki.com.

Spring Cleaning

Wash Windows

Purge Cabinet

DOWNSTAIRS

BEDROOM
ROOM

Spring Cleaning

CRAFT ROOM
MASTER BEDROOM
ROOM
UPSTAIRS
KITCHEN
G ROOM
AIRS   R ROOM

Spring Cleaning

Wash Windows

Purge Cabinet

008
MAKE IT YOURSELF

The ingredients listed in item 007 (and a few more handy items) can be combined in a number of ways to make everything from furniture polish to glass cleaner to disinfectant, and more. These common household items are also inexpensive and often sold in bulk, so you can save money and extra trips to the store by combining them to make your own cleaners. My favorite all-natural recipes are included in the chapter in which they are used, as well as in a master list at the back of this book.

007
RAID YOUR PANTRY

All-natural, homemade cleaning products work wonderfully and smell great. Best of all, they are safe for kids, the home, and the environment. Avoid relying on toxic, potentially harmful chemical solutions and turn to your pantry instead. It is a trove of environmentally friendly ingredients to be used as a foundation for homemade cleaning solutions.

BAKING SODA This natural ingredient is a cleaning and deodorizing workhorse, especially effective in eliminating offensive smells. It's also a mild abrasive.

DISTILLED WHITE VINEGAR Despite its strong scent, vinegar reigns supreme as an excellent cleaner. Add a couple of drops of essential oil (lemon and clove are my favorite combination) to tone down the smell.

LEMON JUICE Add this miracle ingredient to homemade recipes to eliminate odors, remove stains, freshen, and deodorize.

SALT An inexpensive pantry staple, salt can be used to clean many things in the home. Add ¼ c. salt and hot water to burnt pans, let them soak, and then scour away!

LIQUID CASTILE SOAP This great multipurpose cleaner, originally from centuries ago in Spain's Castile region, uses olive oil as its base and is still considered one of the best and most popular natural cleaners today. My favorite castile scent is almond.

Quick Tip

SHAKE IT

To make a handy baking soda sprinkle jar, fill a clean cheese shaker—or a glass jar with holes punched through the lid—with baking soda and sprinkle away.

009

CREATE DIY CLEANERS

Common pantry items can be combined into natural, non-toxic cleaners that can be used throughout the house. Take the time to create your own products with these recipes and you'll be ready for everyday spills.

ALL-PURPOSE CLEANER 2 tsp. borax, ¼ tsp. liquid castile soap, 10 drops lemon essential oil.

Mix all ingredients with hot water in a 16-oz. spray bottle.

ALL-PURPOSE FLOOR CLEANER 1 tsp. almond castile soap, ¼ c. distilled white vinegar, 10 drops orange essential oil, 10 drops clove essential oil.

Mix all ingredients with hot water in a 24-oz. spray bottle.

DISINFECTANT 2 Tbsp. liquid castile soap, 20 drops tea tree oil.

Mix the soap and essential oil with hot water in a 16-oz. spray bottle.

GLASS CLEANER
¼ c. distilled white vinegar, 5 drops lemon essential oil.

Mix all ingredients with hot water in a 16-oz. spray bottle.

NONABRASIVE VINEGAR CLEANER
1 part distilled white vinegar, 2 parts water, 5 drops lavender essential oil.

Combine the vinegar and water in a 16-oz. spray bottle. Add 5 drops of essential oils if you don't like the smell of vinegar—my favorites are lavender, grapefruit, orange, lemon, and peppermint.

010
GET READY TO CLEAN

Cleaning isn't always fun. But you can make it more enjoyable with a plan and a willingness to get it done! Before you begin, imagine it's all finished and your home looks how you've always wanted it. Doesn't that feel good? Don't fret over the time it will take to dust thblinds just put on cleaning clothes, turn up the music, and get to work. Before you know it, you'll be done.

011
LOOK AT THE BIG PICTURE

In the rest of this book, we're going to tackle housecleaning room by room, looking at how to handle these spaces one at a time. But, of course, some things exist in almost every room, or at least in most of them: windows, window coverings, floors, doors, and so on. In the pages that follow, you'll find solutions for these common elements of the home.

012
IMPROVE YOUR OUTLOOK

When was the last time you gave your windows any attention? Last week? Last month? Last year? Your windows need cleaning twice a year. A plan and the right tools will prevent it from being an overwhelming job. Washing the outside may work best as a weekend project, but you can divide the inside by room or a goal-oriented number of windows for each session. Chances are that when you finally get started, you'll wind up cleaning more than your goal. For best results, plan to clean while the sun is not directly shining on the glass, since heat can dry the solution quickly, causing streaks. Here's how to do it right.

STEP ONE Spray the Glass Cleaner solution (see item 009) on the glass. Vinegar breaks down the dingy film that may have built up on the panes, minimizing streaks.

STEP TWO Moving from top to bottom, wipe with a dry microfiber cloth. (It is important that the cloth is lint free, which all microfiber

cloths are.) On inside windows that are not especially dirty, microfiber cloths make quick work of wiping away dirt and drying the glass.

STEP THREE To squeegee or not? Professional window cleaners swear by a squeegee as the fastest and most practical method, particularly for outside windows that take on more grime. Think of how well they work to clean your car windshield! On smaller divided-light windows, pull down from top to bottom. On larger sheets of glass, use horizontal swipes starting at the top. After each run, brush the squeegee with a rag to wipe away the dirt and water. Finish with the microfiber cloth: Use an index finger tucked into a dry spot to go over edges and corners and to dry the wood frame.

013
WIPE DOWN WINDOWS AND MIRRORS

Spray windows and mirrors with the Glass Cleaner (see item 009) and wipe clean with a lint-free microfiber cloth. Avoid using newspaper as a cleaning tool. This advice worked once upon a time, and you'll still see it in some classic cleaning guides, but modern paper and dyes tend to leave smudgy streaks that require extra work to eliminate.

014

FRESHEN UP WINDOW COVERINGS

Over time, dust and dirt may creep their way into your window treatments without being immediately noticeable. To nip this problem in the bud, make it part of your routine to regularly vacuum window treatments inside and out with a dust-brush attachment, and spot-clean as needed. Once or twice a year (depending on the dust level), take them down, bring them outside, and shake them thoroughly. Wash or professionally clean window coverings as needed.

015

CLEAN BLINDS AND SHUTTERS

Since tending to them thoroughly can typically add a lot more time to our cleaning routines, blinds and shutters get overlooked more often than not. Be sure to give them the attention they need whenever you clean, and get into the habit of properly cleaning them monthly.

SPOT CLEAN Using the All-Purpose Cleaner (see item 009) and a microfiber cloth or a specialty tool designed to clean blinds and shutters, wipe away dirt as needed.

DUST MONTHLY Using a vacuum dust-brush attachment on the lowest setting, suction the dirt away. Glide the brush attachment horizontally (not vertically) along the blinds or shutters. Start at the top and move your way down, then reverse the blades and dust on the other side.

DEEP CLEAN If the dust has turned to gunk (as often happens in the kitchen, where steam and grease are in the air), it's time for a more thorough cleaning on removable blinds. Pull the blinds up all the way before lifting them off their supports, and they will be easier to transport. Using a soft sponge, briefly soak and wash them in the bathtub to remove grime. Rinse well, then lay them out on towels to completely dry before rehanging them.

016

STAY ON THE SHADY SIDE

Whether your home has honeycomb, roman, balloon, or roller shades, they need to be cleaned regularly. And it's simpler than you might think! Keep the dust at bay and regularly attend to them to avoid the need for more intense cleaning later.

DUST Completely lower the shades, and dust from top to bottom on both sides using the dust-brush attachment with the vacuum's suction on its lowest level. Covering the attachment with a thin fabric, such as cheesecloth or hosiery, will keep the suction from grabbing the fabric.

SPOT CLEAN If you need to spot-clean fabric shades, test an area in a

lower fold that doesn't show when the shades are partially pulled up. Dampen the area (do not saturate) and gently scrub with a solution of dish soap and water. Use a wet cloth to remove soap residue.

AIR OUT Consider occasionally taking shades down to hang on a line outside for a fresh breath of air.

DRY CLEAN Delicate fabrics, such as silk and wool, need to go to a dry cleaner for a professional cleaning.

017

DEAL WITH DRAPERIES

Your vacuum's versatile dust-brush attachment isn't just for hard surfaces or blinds. It also works well on draperies. Here's a quick and easy

way to keep those draperies fresh and clean with minimal effort.

STEP ONE Dust the top first. If there is a valance, pelmet, or cornice, be sure to first vacuum the top and sides, which are total dust magnets.

STEP TWO Whenever a vacuum is used to clean fabrics, it should be positioned on the lowest setting to prevent damage to the fabric.

STEP THREE Look down. Pay attention to where the curtain hits the floor; dust bunnies love to hide there and accumulate.

STEP FOUR Smell the fabric. Curtains absorb smells and smoke, so even if they appear clean, a more thorough cleaning may be in order.

Quick Tip

CONSIDER DRY CLEANING

If you bought curtains at a big-box store, read the care tag and clean accordingly. If there is no care tag or they were custom made, consider a dry cleaner, especially if they are silk, wool, or another delicate fabric. If the draperies are lined, the lining may shrink with washing. Dry cleaning drapery panels can be costly but will extend their life. Shorter, casual styles, such as cafe curtains, or unlined cotton draperies may be better suited to machine-washing.

018

REMEMBER DOORS AND BASEBOARDS

It's amazing how quickly your doors and baseboards collect dust. But once you add baseboard maintenance to your routine, the process will go surprisingly fast. A duster or a small dust-brush attachment on a vacuum will make this task easier on your back. For resistant dirt, especially in the kitchen where grease settles, use the All-Purpose Cleaner (see item 009) and scrub with a microfiber cloth. A toothbrush also helps for getting crud out of corners.

019

SWIPE THE SWITCH PLATES

Dirty fingers touch the switch plates several times a day. That alone should be enough to inspire you to regularly clean them. Slightly dampen a microfiber cloth with the All-Purpose Cleaner and wipe away the grime. Disposable wipes will suffice when time is limited.

020
REACH
FOR CEILINGS
AND WALLS

Nab cobwebs by using a duster with an extension wand weekly. For a deeper cleaning, use your vacuum's dust-brush attachment, working from ceiling to floor so dust doesn't fall and cling to areas you've just cleaned. Though it may not be visibly apparent, the air circulation from HVAC units deposits fine dust all over walls. Wipe the walls at least once a year to get rid of this fine coating, or every season if your house is a dust magnet!

And remember that not all walls are created equal. High-gloss enamel paint and washable wallpaper are a breeze to clean, while latex paint and fine wallpaper beg for special care. The information here will help you sort through the right process for your particular walls.

Quick Tip

CLEAN WASHABLE
WALLPAPER

You're essentially washing a vinyl coating, so you can treat it as you would a painted wall. Squirt a little detergent in warm water and wipe, then rinse with a damp cloth. Be sure to wipe any excess water to prevent water dripping behind baseboards.

021
KNOW
YOUR PAINTS

The kind of paint, enamel or latex, dictates the appropriate cleaning method. Enamel, or oil-based, paints stand up to daily wear and tougher cleaning than latex paints. That's why enamel paints are popular in kitchens, baths, and play areas. Both enamel and latex paints are available in a full range of finishes ranging from high-gloss, semigloss, satin, and eggshell to flat. Generally, the glossier the paint, the easier it is to wipe away dirt and remove crayon drawings. At the opposite end of the spectrum is a flat finish, which is easily marked and can tolerate only very limited cleaning methods. Eggshell and satin finishes gradually increase in glossiness but are still delicate.

022

KEEP FINE WALLPAPER BEAUTIFUL

To protect the color and pattern you love, regular vacuuming with a soft dust brush is the safest way to keep the paper clean. Save the water for smudges and noticeable dirt. Wetting wallpaper with water or cleaning solution can degrade the paper and weaken the adhesive. Scrubbing will remove the paper along with the stain! The golden rule for cleaning wallpaper is to use only a little moisture and light pressure. Use the following process for treating stains.

HOLD THE WATER Before applying any water, first test a small area in an inconspicuous place and leave it overnight to see if it dries without discoloring the paper or leaving a water spot. If water does not harm the paper, start with a barely damp sponge and gently wipe the soiled area to remove the dirt. Try a mildly soapy water solution if needed. Wipe it over the stain and let it dry before you wipe it again. This may seem tedious, but a slow process guards against fading or tearing wet paper.

APPLY CAREFULLY A thick paste of baking soda and water (as little water as needed to make a paste) is the last resort but can be effective if used carefully. Smear it over the stain and let it rest for a few minutes. Stand by with a dry cloth beneath the paste so you can catch any water before it drips down the wall, then softly wipe the paste off with a damp cloth. You may need to repeat it several times; just make sure the wallpaper never gets too saturated.

ASK GRANDMA One cleaning method for wallpaper stains is an old household trick your grandmother may have used. Roll a slice of white or rye bread into a ball and use it as a natural eraser to remove stains. Dab it on the stain; don't rub. The gluten in the bread absorbs dirt and stains.

023

RESTORE WOOD PANELING

Most wood paneling has a factory coating to protect it, but it still will need regular dusting with a vacuum, feather duster, or microfiber cloth. Wood in family rooms where there's a lot of activity and a fireplace will call for a more intensive seasonal cleaning. Use this process for sealed wood paneling.

STEP ONE Add 1 tsp. mild dishwashing detergent to 24 oz warm water in a spray bottle. Spray on walls, wiping with a slightly damp microfiber cloth as you go.

STEP TWO Mix ½ c. vinegar in 1 gallon warm water. Wet a microfiber cloth in the solution, wringing out as much water as possible. Wipe the paneling to remove any soap residue.

STEP THREE Dry walls with a clean microfiber cloth.

STEP FOUR Polish by putting a small amount of jojoba oil on a microfiber cloth and buffing to a shine.

024

HANDLE WITH CARE

Don't use water on unfinished wood walls! They should be dusted and vacuumed regularly to keep dirt from building up.

Waxed or oiled woods will require special care. Regular dusting with a vacuum attachment or a microfiber cloth is essential. Periodically wipe them down with a soft cloth dipped in warm water and wrung almost dry. Change the cloth often and work right behind yourself to immediately dry the wood with a towel. Reapply the same type of wax or oil after cleaning.

025
SPOT-CLEAN WALLS

Walls, children, and crayons and markers seem to have a special relationship that can try your patience, even if it is momentarily charming. Walls attract all sorts of other stains, such as grease, scuffs, soot, food, mold, and mildew. Here are reliable methods for getting rid of them and restoring your walls to their previous pristine appearance. Refer to the chart for targeted cleaning solutions, but be sure to test in an inconspicuous spot first!

STAIN	SURFACE	WHAT TO DO
Crayon	Painted wall*	Dab white paste toothpaste (no gels) on the stain. Let it rest for a few minutes. Rinse off with a damp microfiber cloth. Dry.
	Nonwashable wallpaper	Use an art gum eraser to get rid of the stain.
Pencil or Pen	Painted wall*	Make a paste of baking soda and water. Rub the paste onto a microfiber cloth. Wipe stain. Rinse off. Remove paste completely. Dry.
	Nonwashable wallpaper	Use an art gum eraser to get rid of the stain.
Black Marks	Painted wall*	Dab white paste toothpaste (no gels) on the stain. Let it rest for a few minutes. Rinse off with a damp microfiber cloth. Dry.
Fingerprints	Washable or nonwashable wallpaper	Roll a piece of bread rolled into a ball, or an art gum eraser, over the mark.
Grease Spots	Washable wallpaper	Mix talcum powder or cornstarch with a bit of water to make a paste on a microfiber cloth. Apply to stain. Let it rest for 10 minutes. Rinse with water (not too much). Dry.
	Nonwashable wallpaper	Hold a thick paper bag or layers of paper towels over the stain, and briefly press with an iron on a low-heat setting. The grease should adhere to the paper.

*Works on glossy enamel paint, but test carefully before trying on any latex paint or on flat, eggshell, or satin enamel.

026
CARE FOR EXPOSED BRICK

It may not show dirt because of its rough surface and dark color, but exposed brick gets dirty just like any other wall. Brick is porous, so soot from a fireplace, as well as dirt and dust, find a welcome spot to roost. Regularly dust brick with a microfiber cloth or the dust-brush attachment on the vacuum cleaner.

STEP ONE Mix one part salt to one part mild dishwashing liquid or castile soap. Add just enough water to make a thick paste.

STEP TWO Apply the mixture to the wall, which may be easiest to do with your hands. Scrub the wall with a stiff scrub brush and leave the paste on for 10 minutes.

STEP THREE Remove the paste with a clean wet sponge. Rinse the sponge often in a bucket of clean water to remove any trace of the paste and its residue as you work. If the paste adheres to the brick, use a clean scrub brush to get it off.

027
MAKE A GRAND ENTRANCE

Exterior doors must be seasonally cleaned. Outside doors take a beating—weather, dirty hands, spills, kicks, and more. It's going to happen. However, they are an introduction to your home, so you want doors to be as clean as possible. A door's materials govern your cleaning strategy, so use these tips for the most common door materials.

WOOD A solution of castile soap and water applied with a microfiber cloth will thoroughly clean the door and door surround. Start at the top, attacking tough stains, scuffs, or dirt with the cloth while being careful not to scratch paint or damage the decorative finish.

SLIDING GLASS Fingerprints and smudges stick out like a sore thumb on glass doors but are easily eliminated with the Glass Cleaner (see item 009). However, the slider tracks catch all sorts of crud, bugs, and spills that can eventually impede the mechanics of the doors. Use the vacuum's crevice attachment to dispose of dirt and debris in the track every time you vacuum the room's floor. A toothbrush may be needed to dislodge resistant gunk trapped in the tracks. The glass and metal frame should follow the window-cleaning schedule twice a year.

FIBERGLASS OR PAINTED STEEL Wipe clean with a soft cloth and mild soapy water.

028
DON'T FORGET THE BIN

No matter how meticulous you are about using trash bags, things of unknown origin will make it to the bottom of the can. The key is to regularly clean it before the grime builds up! Put on gloves and take the can outside or put it in the shower. Thoroughly rinse it with hot, soapy water and use a scrub brush to dislodge stubborn gunk. Rinse and let it dry. Air-drying in the sun naturally disinfects, but spraying with the Disinfectant (see item 009) is still recommended.

029
GET HANDS-ON

Doorknobs transfer germs and bacteria from person to person. Add cleaning them to your monthly chore list to keep knobs sparkling clean. To help eliminate the spread of illness, disinfect weekly during winter months, when colds and viruses run rampant. Spray a microfiber cloth with the Disinfectant (see item 009) and then thoroughly scrub each doorknob in your house.

OLD COPPER, BRASS, AND BRONZE These knobs tend to tarnish over time, so special care is needed if you want them to look new again. However, if you're a preservationist or nostalgist (like me), you may prefer the tarnished look. In any case, regularly clean them to remove dirt and grime. To clean, dampen a cloth with the Disinfectant and thoroughly wipe the knob. Dry and buff with a second microfiber cloth, taking care not to leave any moisture or disinfectant behind.

To polish copper and brass, mix 2 Tbsp. salt with just enough lemon juice to make a thick paste. Rub it on and let stand for 30 minutes. Wash off with a cloth dampened with soapy water, and rinse with a clean damp cloth and dry. For bronze, use 2 Tbsp. baking soda with lemon juice to make a paste, and follow the same instructions.

NEW FINISHES New hardware is often treated with a lacquer finish to hold its high polish. Regularly clean it, but do not apply any polishing paste, or risk stripping off the protective lacquer (unless it begins to tarnish, which signals that it lacks a lacquer finish).

NICKEL, CHROME, STAINLESS STEEL, AND OIL-RUBBED BRONZE Knobs are available in an abundance of finishes, including options for polished or brushed (also called satin finish). The Disinfectant is a combination of all-natural products and should be safe for any of these finishes, but if in doubt, check with the manufacturer.

CRYSTAL AND GLASS Crystal is easy to care for. Carefully wash with warm, soapy water and a soft cloth and immediately dry with a cotton towel to prevent water spots.

030

START AT THE BOTTOM

I love walking into a room with clean and shiny floors. Who doesn't? Maintaining floors daily makes the entire house feel cleaner (even if it really isn't!). So take a few minutes every day and clean them. If you don't have time to deep-clean, no problem. Quickly cover the high-traffic areas with your vacuum, as vacuuming picks up more dust and debris than sweeping or dust mopping. Spot-clean messes before they harden with a damp microfiber cloth. A quick daily cleaning will remove dirt, twigs, small stones, and other hard debris that get tracked inside and will scratch any floor if not quickly removed. This is your first line of defense.

MOVE FAST If spills are immediately addressed, there's less likelihood of tough spots. Wipe with a damp cloth and dry with another cloth. When tackling a particularly difficult stain, remember that the top priority is preventing floor damage.

WATCH THE WATER Too much water can damage almost all flooring materials. Be thorough, but use a light touch when it comes to liquids. Never mop without first sweeping or vacuuming to remove debris that will scratch with swipes of the mop.

LOSE THE SHOES Eliminate dirty floors at the source by implementing a "no shoes" rule. The primary reason floors get dirty is people wearing shoes in the house. If you have a medical issue and need to wear them, designate a clean pair that you can switch to when you get home, or wear slippers.

031

USE A SPRAY MOP

Streamline floor cleaning by switching out your old-school, germ-filled mop and bucket of water with a spray mop. It saves a lot of time and money, and it's more sanitary.

Look for a spray mop that allows you to mist a floor cleaning solution onto the floor just ahead of the flathead microfiber pad. Microfiber pads can be laundered (without bleach or fabric softener), and even disposable refills can be washed several times before tossing. This application is not only easier, but is more sanitary than wringing out an old-fashioned cotton mop head. Also avoid mops or sweepers that require same-brand disposable sheets, which often have toxic chemicals.

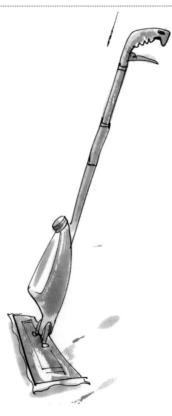

Quick Tip

AVOID COSTLY MISTAKES

Though cleaning practices for many flooring materials are similar, using the wrong technique or cleaner can be disastrous. Be sure that you know exactly which kind of flooring is installed in each room before doing any intensive cleaning. Some floors, such as hardwood, can take on a hazy or cloudy film if not treated properly, or even become warped if too much water is absorbed. Scrubbing your laminate, bamboo, or wooden floors too firmly can scuff them or wear off the finish. Concrete and some stone and tile floors are porous and can absorb harsh cleansers, leading to permanent stains or color changes.

032 FIND THE RIGHT FLOOR SOLUTION

Opinions about what works best to clean floors differ, but I've found that homemade, natural cleaning solutions are the best option for me. They are healthier for my family, gentler on my floors, inexpensive, and simply better for the environment. I've created several homemade spray-mop solutions that can be used throughout the home. Don't waste another cent buying premade, expensive floor cleaners! If you are unsure whether a cleaning solution is right for your floors, spot-test, or ask your flooring manufacturer. Feel free to swap in your favorite essential oils to create a personalized scent!

ALL-PURPOSE FLOOR CLEANER

1 tsp. almond castile soap, ¼ c. distilled white vinegar, 10 drops orange essential oil, 10 drops clove essential oil.

Mix in a 24-oz. spray bottle with hot water.

HARDWOOD FLOOR CLEANER

1 tsp. almond castile soap and 10 drops lemon essential oil.

Mix in a 24-oz. spray bottle with hot water. Use sparingly to minimize the chance of warping; do not use on unsealed hardwoods.

LAMINATE FLOOR CLEANER

¾ c. distilled white vinegar, ¾ c. rubbing alcohol, 10 drops peppermint essential oil.

Mix in a 24-oz. spray bottle with ¾ c. hot water. Use sparingly to minimize the chance of warping.

TILE FLOOR CLEANER

¼ c. distilled white vinegar and 15 drops orange essential oil.

Mix in a 24-oz. spray bottle with hot water.

VINYL FLOOR CLEANER

¼ c. distilled white vinegar, 3 Tbsp. borax, 10 drops lemon essential oil, 10 drops lavender essential oil.

Mix in a 24-oz. spray bottle with hot water.

033

HANDLE HARDWOOD

Most hardwood floors are sealed with a urethane finish, but not all. Sticklers for historic authenticity may prefer not to seal heartpine or other original wood that has developed a patina over time. A urethane coating on your hardwood floor extends the time between refinishings, but your diligence in cleaning will also be a factor. Polyurethane is essentially a plastic coat intended to maintain a comparatively carefree, long-term finish, and there's a long list of products that will etch and dull the finish. Never use an oil soap, acrylic "mop and shine" products, paste or liquid wax, vinegar, or ammonia, and avoid abrasive rubbing. Steam cleaning is not recommended, as it may damage the coating and the wood beneath.

DO IT DAILY For daily cleaning, use a microfiber dust mop or vacuum. A slightly damp mop is okay, if the floor is immediately dried.

CLEAN SEALED FLOORS To do a deeper clean of a sealed floor, fill a spray bottle with the Hardwood Floor Cleaner (see item 032) and mist a 4' x 4' section. Mop back and forth along the grain of the wood (following the length of the boards) to minimize streaking, then continue to another section.

CARE FOR OILED WOOD Regular cleaning is even more imporant here because a penetrating oil finish protects wood from drying but will allow stains to penetrate. Vacuum often and mop with clear water once a week. Avoid excess moisture when mopping, and do not steam clean this type of flooring. Never use ammonia, detergents, soaps, or commercial cleaners.

HOLD THE WATER ON WAX If your floors have a waxed finish instead of a polyurethane seal, vacuum them with the floor brush. Water will damage wax, so use a damp cloth to immediately wipe up spills.

034
USE A LIGHT TOUCH ON BAMBOO

Too much grit or too much water will damage this renewable, eco-friendly material. Bamboo is prone to scratching from every-day dirt that gets tracked into the house. Sweep daily, but use a soft-bristled broom or micro-fiber dust mop, or vacuum with the floor-brush attachment. Mop weekly with the Hardwood Floor Cleaner (see item 032) by misting a small area and following with a mi-crofiber mop. Don't let the cleaner pool on the floor. Avoid ammonia, vinegar, and other acidic cleaners.

035
KEEP LAMINATES LOVELY

Laminate floors are made from a remarkable likeness of wood flooring encased in a plastic laminate to get the look of hardwood without the cost and care. However, laminate floors cannot be refinished, so it's especially important to take good care of them.

SPOT TREATMENT For daily cleaning, use a microfiber mop or vacuum. For more thorough cleaning, spray the Laminate Floor Cleaner (see item 032) onto a mop and work in small sections. Immediately wash off with a damp mop, and thoroughly dry with a towel.

USE CAUTION Never use a wet mop, as water can seep into seams, loosening the laminate and damaging the wood-fiber backing. Abrasive cleaners and applicators will scratch laminates, while soap, detergents, acrylic "mop and shine" products, waxing, and polishing will damage the factory finish. As with wood floors, avoid steam cleaning.

037
CARE FOR CORK

A naturally sustainable and nontoxic material, cork is also resilient, making it easier on the feet and back than many other surfaces. It is quite porous, so all cork flooring must be sealed. The sealant applied to cork is a thin coat, and tiny particles that aren't visible will scratch it, so be meticulous in daily cleaning with a broom, microfiber dust mop, or vacuum floor attachment.

MOP CLEAN Use a damp mop only with the All-Purpose Floor Cleaner (see item 032). Avoid saturating with water. If cork hasn't air-dried by the time you finish mopping, dry it with a clean towel. Never use any commercial product on cork, or abrasive sponges that can scratch right through the thin seal on top of the cork.

GET THE JUMP ON SPILLS Never give spills a chance to soak in—immediately wipe up as much as possible. Spray with the All-Purpose Floor Cleaner (see item 032), rubbing gently with a microfiber cloth. Rinse with clean water and dry with a towel.

036
PAMPER STONE

Just as silk blouses need a little special handling, so do natural stone floors. Liquids can penetrate stone; a protective sealant, generally applied at installation, boosts stain resistance but won't make a floor stainproof.

DAILY CARE Daily removal of dirt and grit is as critical for stone as it is for any floor. Ground underfoot by walking, tiny particles will scratch. A dry microfiber mop minimizes chances of scratching.

KEEP IT CLEAN Use a damp mop with clean water only, changing the water often. Dry the floor with a towel or a microfiber pad to prevent water spots. Seasonally and after a widespread spill, mop using the Tile Floor Cleaner (see item 032), then rinse thoroughly with clean water before drying the floor.

FIGHT STAINING Quickly blot a liquid spill with a dry cloth to absorb as much as possible. Dampen a white cloth with a mild soap-and-water solution and briefly tamp the stain until it stops appearing on the cloth. Don't saturate the area. Rinse with clear water and dry with a cloth. Even water leaves stains if left long enough. Wine, colas, and acidic foods react with stone—clean them up fast! Avoid abrasive brushes or sponges and ammonia-based cleaners.

038
GET A CONCRETE SOLUTION

Concrete, long used as an industrial flooring, has recently become popular inside the house as well. Naturally porous, it should be sealed for easy maintenance—although the sealant only makes it stain resistant, not stainproof. It is possible to seal an existing concrete floor, but it's a job best left to professionals. Daily cleaning doesn't require anything special beyond the basics.

SOAP AND RINSE Never use ammonia or vinegar on concrete, as they can damage the sealant. To make a natural cleaning solution for concrete, mix 1 tsp. of mild soap (my favorite is a citrus castile soap) into a gallon of warm water. Work in small sections with a damp mop, frequently dipping the mop and wringing out as much soapy water as possible. Then make another run over the floor, using clean water to remove soap residue.

TREAT SPILLS Any substance that might stain cannot be allowed to sit. Immediately clean spills with a castile soap solution. If the stain is still apparent, leave the solution on for 20 minutes and scrub with a stiff-bristle brush.

039
LOVE THAT LINOLEUM

Everything old is new again, and homeowners who might once have ripped out linoleum floors are finding a new appreciation for its retro-cool designs and easy care. Made from organic materials (primarily linseed oil, plus a number of additives such as cork, pine resin, and minerals), it is antibacterial and nonallergenic.

Linoleum can be swept or vacuumed like most floors; for more thorough cleaning, use a spray mop that's been dampened with the All-Purpose Floor Cleaner (see item 032) or spray a small section of the floor at a time, just big enough that you can mop it right away. Treat tougher spots by dampening a cloth with the All-Purpose Floor Cleaner and gently rubbing the mark.

Never use strong alkaline cleaners, such as ammonia, bleach, or hydrogen peroxide.

040

TREAT TILES RIGHT

As with wood floors, tiles also come in a wide range of materials and finishes. Whether they're made of ceramic or porcelain, flooring tiles can be either glazed or polished, or unglazed. Daily care is the same for all these surfaces, but use the right techniques for anything beyond the basics (by which we mean sweeping, cleaning with a microfiber dust mop, or using the floor attachment for your vacuum). Tile is almost always grouted; for grout-cleaning techniques, see item 005.

CERAMIC OR PORCELAIN TILES	TO WASH	SPOT TREATMENT	BE CAREFUL
GLAZED OR POLISHED	Damp-mop with the Tile Floor Cleaner (see item 032) and dry it using a second microfiber cloth or another mop to avoid leaving any water spots and streaking.	Opt for a soft-bristled toothbrush to avoid scratching the finish. Use a small amount of the Tile Floor Cleaner on tough stains, but immediately remove the cleaner with a damp cloth or a mop and hot water.	This is no place for scrub brushes and stiff bristles, as they will scratch the polished finish. Ammonia and bleach are no-no's that can discolor the tile and grout.
UNGLAZED	Saturate a small area, 3 or 4 feet, with the Tile Floor Cleaner and, after a few minutes, wipe away. Then, follow up with a clean, dry microfiber cloth to remove moisture, working in manageable sections.	Unglazed tiles are very porous, so any stain must immediately be cleaned before it can sink into the tile. Scrape or wipe up at once, and if needed, scrub the area with a toothbrush.	Don't let water or other liquid sit on the surface. Water stains can easily develop, and the unglazed tile can become a home for mold or mildew.

041

MAINTAIN A VINYL FLOOR

Soft underfoot and easy to maintain, vinyl comes in sheet form and tiles. The tiles may imitate ceramic tiles, natural stone, or wood. Quality, or grading, considerably varies. What does not vary is how simple, regular cleaning is essential to prolonging the floor's life. Nothing fancy is necessary for daily cleaning, just the basic broom, microfiber dust mop, or proper vacuum cleaner attachment.

MOP IT UP Dampen a mop with clean water and spray with the Vinyl Floor Cleaner (see item 032). The vinegar will cut through grease and disinfect, while the essential oils will restore shine.

TREAT SCUFFS Vinyl will scuff, but gently rubbing with a bit of liquid wax like jojoba will remove scuffs. Then apply the Vinyl Floor Cleaner to remove the oil. Spot-clean food stains with a toothbrush and a paste of baking soda and water, rinsing well with clean water.

PROLONG THE FLOOR'S LIFE Abrasive cleaners and applicators will scratch vinyl, and soap, detergents, and acrylic "mop and shine" products will dull the finish. Ammonia will likely cause cracks in the surface, and paste waxes or solvent-based polishes can damage the material.

042

CHECK YOUR CARPETS AND RUGS

Before you put any cleaner on a rug or carpet, find out what kind of fiber it's made of: wool, silk, cotton, another natural fiber, or synthetic. Cleaning techniques and stain-removal guidelines differ. It's always a good idea to consult the owner's manual or manufacturer's website if you have any questions, but here are some basics on the most common materials.

WOOL Perhaps the most durable and resilient of fibers, wool nevertheless has a few specific quirks. When vacuuming, make certain the beater bar—the spinning bar under the vacuum attachment that lifts dirt and hair off the ground—is set on "high" so that it barely brushes against the top of the fibers. Overly aggressive beating can lead to pilling when it comes to wool. Instead of instinctively paralleling the edge of the rug with the vacuum, try a V-shaped trajectory that prevents crushing the fibers. Also, go slowly to give the vacuum enough time to suck up all the dust.

SILK Both silk rugs and silk patterns woven within a wool rug will require caution when cleaning. Treat stains with lukewarm water only. Try using the upholstery-brush attachment instead of the beater bar, which can change the texture of a silk rug.

PLANT FIBERS Plant-based natural-fiber rugs, such as sisal, seagrass, jute, and hemp, are favorites for their natural texture and casual good looks. With the exception of seagrass, which is water resistant and therefore more stain resistant, natural-fiber rugs will readily absorb water and stains. Blot—don't rub—any spill with a microfiber cloth or clean white towel. Even water, if not removed immediately, can mix with the dirt in a rug and create a dark stain. Scrape up any solid substance with a spoon and let the rest dry. Gently brush and vacuum to remove the rest.

Natural fibers need more frequent vacuuming than most rugs, as dirt will cut into the fibers when ground in by foot traffic. Instead of the beater bar on your vacuum, consider using an upholstery-brush or dust-brush attachment. Both are softer and better suited to getting between tight weaves. Move the vacuum back and forth on the length of the rug and then vacuum again from side to side. Working in both directions picks up dirt trapped in the weave.

SYNTHETICS Artificially made, synthetic fibers are inherently stain resistant. Though you still need to quickly respond to stains, you'll find them much easier to remove in comparison to natural fibers.

043

PRESERVE AN ANTIQUE RUG

Antique rugs have held up to decades, if not centuries, of wear. With proper care, you can keep your antique rug in great condition for the next generation.

SHAKE IT OFF Shake out the rug if it's small enough. Carpets absorb odors and dust. It's a good idea to expose the rug to air at least once a year, but avoid putting it in direct sunlight. Rotate the rug once or twice during the year to evenly distribute wear from too traffic.

VACUUM CAREFULLY Always vacuum on the lowest suction setting. Stay away from the fringe; you risk damaging it if it gets sucked into the attachment. If a lower setting is not an option, sweep with a broom. With either method, turn the rug over and clean both the front and back.

044
SIZE UP AN AREA RUG

The rug world has exploded with all manner of graphic, modern, and traditional designs. With so many handsome possibilities available, design leaders will now often layer area rugs on top of larger carpets. Take care of your smaller rugs, and they'll eventually become beautiful vintage treasures.

KEEP IT CLEAN Vacuum both the front and back of the rug as well as the floor or carpet underneath. If possible, shake the rug outside to dislodge resistant dirt.

DO THE WASH You may be able to put a small cotton or synthetic rug in the washing machine set on the gentle cycle. Check the care tag before washing. Protect the colors from fading by air-drying as soon as possible after washing.

045
CARE FOR COWHIDE

Cowhide rugs have really caught on, in part because of their easy maintenance. Vacuum in the direction that the hair falls, using an upholstery-brush attachment rather than a beater bar. Move quickly to clean up spills with warm soapy water, but don't saturate the hide.

046
SAVE THE SHEEPSKIN

Be gentle when washing a sheepskin rug, cleaning it in a way that is safe for both the leather pelt and the long, luxurious sheepskin fibers. If you don't specifically know that you can machine-wash your sheepskin rug, hand-wash it in a sink or bathtub.

Brush the rug using a sheepskin carding brush—a tool with long metal bristles—and then shake the rug out to remove as much dirt as possible before washing it in cold water with a mild liquid detergent. Do not use wool washes or laundry detergents, particularly ones that include enzymes or bleach. Swish the rug gently in the water without scrubbing to avoid matting.

Drain and refill the sink or tub as often as is needed until the water is running clear. Dry the rug flat afterward, away from direct sunlight and heat; resist trying to hurry the drying proces so as not to harm the rug. Once the rug is fully dried, brush it again with the carding brush.

047
STAY ON TOP OF CARPETS

With wall-to-wall carpet (as well as a large area rug or a throw rug) regular vacuuming is essential to keeping a clean house. Carpets will look fresh and clean, and they'll also last longer. Dirt and grit builds up in carpets and can fray the fibers.

Most carpets need cleaning only once a week (that's every Wednesday for me), but I hit high-traffic areas, such as the foyer and main living spaces, more frequently. And while I'm at it, shaking out smaller rugs is an ancient cleaning method and still satisfying to me. By staying on top of a weekly routine, I need to shampoo carpets only once a year during my spring cleaning.

048
LIFT STAINS NATURALLY

Sometimes a stain needs just a little help to come out, and a little bit of soap and water can lift it right out. For tougher stains, white vinegar will provide a boost that breaks up the staining culprit.

BASIC CARPET STAIN REMOVER

Mix ¼ tsp. castile soap with water in a 16-oz. spray bottle.

VINEGAR-BASED CARPET STAIN REMOVER

Mix 1 Tbsp. castile soap, 1 Tbsp. white vinegar, and 2 c. warm water in a 16-oz. spray bottle.

049
ACT IMMEDIATELY

The inevitable misfortune of a spill or tracked mud is bound to happen. But since my carpets are regularly vacuumed, such a mishap always gets my attention right away before it can permanently stain. Spot-treating carpet stains requires patience and tenacity. It may take repeated treatments to completely clean a stain, but the basic process is always the same.

BLOT THE STAIN Act immediately to absorb as much as possible or scrape up thicker spills with a spoon.

SPRAY IT ONCE Directly apply the appropriate stain remover (see item 048) onto the stain. Be stingy with the amount of solution and water you put on the carpet, though—if the backing gets saturated, it's prone to mildew.

RESIST RUBBING Horizontal motions will only spread the stain. Instead, blot the stain with a damp cloth, moving from the outside of the stain toward the center.

TEST AND REPEAT With a clean spot on the cloth, check to see if the stain transfers to the cloth. If it does or if you can still see the stain on the carpet, repeat spraying and blotting until the stain is gone.

RINSE LIGHTLY Always end with a cold water rinse, spraying the treated spot with clean water and blotting as needed to completely remove all of the cleaning solution.

DRY IT OUT Remove as much moisture as possible with a dry, clean cloth.

050
FIGHT COMMON STAINS NATURALLY

A clean white cotton cloth is the best tool for this job. Use white, as colors might react with your cleaning solvent and bleed into the carpet's fibers. Cotton cloths are the most absorbent, more environmentally friendly, and will not degrade with use.

ID THE STAIN	TREAT IT WELL
TOMATO-BASED SAUCES (E.G. SPAGHETTI SAUCE, KETCHUP, BARBECUE SAUCE)	Start with the Basic Carpet Stain Remover. If the stain is still there, step up to Vinegar-Based Carpet Stain Remover. Rinse.
WINE, JUICE, BERRIES, CHOCOLATE, SODAS	Apply the Vinegar-Based Carpet Stain Remover and repeat as necessary. Rinse.
COFFEE, TEA	Apply the Vinegar-Based Carpet Stain Remover and repeat as necessary. Rinse.
OIL-BASED FOOD (SALAD DRESSINGS, BUTTER, OLIVE OIL)	Immediately sprinkle with baking soda and leave it for 10 minutes to absorb the oil. Vacuum lightly, then apply the Vinegar-Based Carpet Stain Remover as needed. Rinse.
MILK PRODUCTS	Use a spoon and cloth to remove spill from the carpet. Spray with the Basic Carpet Stain Remover. To eliminate a lingering spoiled-dairy smell, sprinkle with baking soda and allow it to sit overnight. Loosen with a dull knife in the morning, and vacuum.
DIRT, SOIL, MUD	Use a spoon or soft brush to remove as much as possible. Apply the Vinegar-Based Carpet Stain Remover and repeat as needed. Rinse.
RED CLAY	Brush away as much as possible with a toothbrush. Put ¼ c. salt in a bowl and add just enough white vinegar to make a paste. Put the paste on the stain and leave for several hours. Rinse, let dry, and vacuum.
URINE	Use successive dry cloths to absorb as much liquid as possible. Mix equal parts white vinegar and water and spray on the carpet. Blot with a white cotton cloth, changing cloths often, and continue until all color is gone. If the stain or odor persists, generously sprinkle baking soda, leave it overnight, then vacuum.
FECES, VOMIT	With gloves, use a spoon or spatula to remove as much as you can from the carpet. Blot any liquid, and apply the Vinegar-Based Stain Remover as needed. Sprinkle baking soda on the spot and let rest for 15 minutes. Vacuum.

051
LIGHT THE WAY

Lighting can change the mood of a room with a flip of a switch, so it's easy to take it for granted—until a bulb burns out or the lamplight dims because the shade is so dusty. Lamps need to be part of your weekly cleaning routine, while other fixtures need attention every six months to a year. When done weekly, lamps take only minutes to clean. Put it off and the job becomes more complicated.

052
BRIGHTEN LAMPSHADES

A quick, light weekly cleaning is essential for preserving your lampshades. By the time you notice a layer of dust or dirt on the lampshade, the only resort may be to toss the shade and buy another. Dust that settles on a shade turns to grime from moisture in the air, discoloring the shade. Heat from the lightbulb accelerates the darkening of a stain on the shade. Devote a few seconds to cleaning your lampshades and enjoy them for a long time.

DUST Dusting is critical with paper shades because they cannot be washed without becoming stained, warped, or damaged. Other shade materials that are attached to the frame with glue instead of stitching will also come apart in water, so keep up with the dusting.

Get into the habit of dusting the lamps and sconces (bulbs, base, and shade) every time you dust a room. Work when the light is off and cool to the touch. A microfiber cloth is best because it will pick up the dust instead of brushing it down onto the table or the floor.

VACUUM If you prefer, clean lampshades when you vacuum. Gently wipe the shade with the dust-brush attachment. Avoid suction directly on the fringe or other decorative trim; slide hosiery over the dust brush to keep from pulling off the trim.

TOOLS You can also use a clean paintbrush (1"–2" wide) or a lint roller to remove dust from the shade. Find a method that is easy for you so you're more likely to do it.

053

WASH A FABRIC LAMPSHADE

Examine your shades before cleaning them, because not all are washable. Fabric shades sewn onto a wire frame can and should be washed at least once a year. Sewn fabric shades, such as cotton, linen, and even silk, can be carefully washed by hand. Plastic shades can be sponged clean with water and mild soap, then completely dried.

It's tricky to spot-clean a fabric lampshade; rubbing one spot can damage the fabric and create a hole. Putting water or soap on one spot may simply replace a stain with a water spot. When you discover a stain, it's often best to clean the entire shade.

STEP ONE Dust first to remove as much dust and dirt as you can.

STEP TWO Fill a bathtub or a deep sink with enough lukewarm water to be able to immerse the shade. Add 1 Tbsp. of castile soap. Don't use dishwashing soap or detergent!

STEP THREE Holding the shade by its wire frame, dip the shade and swirl it gently in the water until it appears clean. Drain the dirty water and refill the tub or sink with cool water. Continue to dip and gently swirl the shade until all soap and dirt is gone. Drain and refill until the water is running clear after rinsing the shade.

STEP FOUR Dry the shade away from direct sunlight. A hairdryer on a cool setting can speed the process; avoid the hot setting.

054

SHINE GLASS SHADES

Sconces often have glass shades; wash these by hand in warm, soapy water once a year. Put towels in the sink to protect the shades, and don't use a dishwasher. Dry completely before returning them to the fixture.

Many pendant lights also have glass shades, especially in the kitchen. If they are not removable, you may need a ladder. Turn the electricity off at the panel. Then clean the shades with a sponge and soapy water from a bucket you can securely take up the ladder with you. Change the water often to remove built-up layers of dirt. Rinse the glass with a clean sponge and a bucket of clear water until the glass is shining.

055

REVIVE THE LAMP BASE

Lamps of all sorts as well as wall and ceiling fixtures can be made from a wide range of materials. Here's how to handle some of the most common ones you'll see.

MYSTERY METALS Many metal lighting fixtures are manufactured with various lacquered, painted, or powder-coated finishes, which can be potentially damaged by cleaning products and scrubbing. When buying a new fixture, ask at the time of purchase how to clean it. Otherwise, it's often a guessing game to identify the finish. If that's the case, wipe it off with clear water on a slightly damp cloth and then immediately dry the metal fixture.

BRASS AND COPPER If tarnish appears, your fixtures don't have a lacquered finish or the finish is breaking down and needs to be stripped. To polish tarnished brass and copper, sprinkle a generous amount of table salt on a lemon half and rub. Use as many lemons as needed to cover the surface. Wash with a mild Wipe with a mild soap and water solution on a soft cloth. Dampen another cloth and rinse soap off, then dry.

WOOD Dust unfinished wood. For stained or varnished woods, apply the Furniture Polish (see item 197) with a soft cloth and buff with a clean cloth. Painted wood just needs a barely damp cloth and clear water; dry quickly with a soft cloth.

056

MAKE CHANDELIERS SPARKLE

Weekly dusting with a microfiber cloth is the best way to keep a chandelier looking good, but often the fixture is not reachable. Opt for a microfiber duster on an extension wand for this delicate work. Once a year, plan on a serious cleaning, either by working on a ladder or by taking the fixture down from the ceiling to work on it. In either case, turn the electricity off at the panel.

SNAP A PICTURE If the chandelier has a complex design, take a few snapshot of it before you take the chandelier apart—you'll be glad you did when you have find a piece that doesn't seem to go anywhere! Spread a drop cloth beneath the work area. Remove all breakable bulbs. Use protective eyewear if you're working from a ladder.

CLIMB A LADDER When cleaning a crystal or glass chandelier while you're on a ladder, spray the Glass Cleaner (see item 009) onto a microfiber cloth and gently wipe the pieces. Never spray cleaner onto the fixture itself! Wipe each crystal and dry with a clean microfiber cloth.

TAKE IT DOWN If you're able to take a crystal or glass chandelier down from the ceiling, this complex project becomes a much easier job. Remove the crystals carefully, paying attention to how they are attached so you can correctly reassemble them when you're done.

057

LOOK UP

Flush-mounted lights need cleaning at least once a year. Remove all but the mounting hardware. Chandeliers require special work (see item 056), but every fixture deserves attention.

CEILING FIXTURES Remove and clean all but the mounting hardware at least once a year. Wash glass by hand in mild, soapy water, rinse well, and dry before reattaching. Clean metal covers with soapy water, just using a sponge or cloth to apply the cleaner, rinse, and dry well before reattaching. If you find moths and insects on the glass fixture, consider taking the fixture down more often for cleaning.

DRUM SHADES Pendant lights with drum shades can be cleaned with the vacuum extension and the dust-brush attachment. If the shade is fabric, follow guidelines in item 053.

Quick Tip

DUST THE BULBS

Gently wiping bulbs with a microfiber cloth greatly increases the amount of light emitted, particularly if you've never done it before.

OVERVIEW
Checklists

It might seem daunting at first glance, but don't be intimidated—this list is just meant to be a guide, a framework of suggestions. Tailor the to-dos to your life: whether or not you have pets, children, a housekeeper, a need to keep things tidy or not. Make the list work for you, according to your reality.

Numbers refer to the general cleaning entries, so make sure to reference the appropriate supporting items to address specific materials and circumstances.

DAILY

- ☐ Whole-house pick up
- ☐ Spot-clean spills and potential stains
- ☐ Sweep or vacuum floors *30*

- ☐ _____
- ☐ _____
- ☐ _____
- ☐ _____

WEEKLY

- ☐ Dust window treatments *14*
- ☐ Dust doors and baseboards *18*
- ☐ Clean switch plates *19*
- ☐ Dust ceilings and walls *20*
- ☐ Mop floors *31*
- ☐ Vacuum carpets and area rugs *42, 44*
- ☐ Dust lampshades and chandeliers *52, 56*

- ☐ _____
- ☐ _____
- ☐ _____
- ☐ _____
- ☐ _____
- ☐ _____
- ☐ _____

MONTHLY

- ☐ Clean mirrors *13*
- ☐ Clean window treatments *14*
- ☐ Wash trash bins *28*
- ☐ Clean doorknobs *29*

- ☐ _____
- ☐ _____
- ☐ _____
- ☐ _____

SEASONALLY (SPRING AND FALL)

- ☐ Wash windows *12*
- ☐ Deep-clean window treatments *14*
- ☐ Wipe doors and baseboards *18*
- ☐ Clean walls *20*
- ☐ Clean exterior doors *27*
- ☐ Deep-clean lampshades *53*
- ☐ Clean lamp bases and sconces *54, 55*
- ☐ Clean chandeliers and fixtures *56, 57*

- ☐ _____
- ☐ _____
- ☐ _____
- ☐ _____
- ☐ _____
- ☐ _____
- ☐ _____
- ☐ _____
- ☐ _____

Kitchen

Our kitchen is the hub of the home.

It's command central, which also means that it's typically the messiest place in the house. Ingredients drip, spices spill, and sauces splatter— this is just part of the process of making healthy meals for your family. It takes time and effort to keep the kitchen clean, and as the saying goes, many hands make light work. So, at the end of every day, our whole family pitches in and quickly cleans up our messes. In this section, you'll find the morning and nighttime routines we follow to help keep our kitchen looking presentable and generally clean. By creating a daily cleaning routine, you can finally wake up to a clean kitchen without the hassle of clearing messes just to eat breakfast. You'll also find essential checklists and valuable tips to conquer those kitchen messes.

058 CARE FOR YOUR KITCHEN

It's the site of food preparation and consumption, homework completion and minor injury triage, intimate conversation and coffee with your besties, so the kitchen must be presentable at all times. From wiping down surfaces every day to deep cleaning appliances seasonally, I'll help you navigate kitchen clean up and make the process hassle free—or at least hassle friendly. In this section are my best practices for cleaning appliances, sinks, counters, and cabinets.

059 COMPLETE YOUR EVENING

It feels great to start the day with a clean kitchen. I'm convinced it boosts my mood for the entire day. So before I go to bed, I do a quick clean up. It should take no more than 15 minutes.

LOAD Fill the dishwasher and start it. Unload first thing in the morning.

WASH Clean anything that can't go in the dishwasher and set it all aside to air-dry.

CLEAN Rinse the sink, sprinkle with baking soda and a squirt of castile soap. With a sponge, work it into a paste and let it sit while you clean the table, counters, and stove.

SPRAY Use the All-Purpose Cleaner (see item 104) on tables, counters, and the stove, and wipe them down.

DRY Go back to the hand-washed pieces, dry with a towel if needed, and put them away.

RINSE Wash the baking soda paste off the sink and polish dry with a clean towel to prevent water spots.

SWEEP Use a broom and dustpan or vacuum to clean the floor.

FRESHEN Put out new washcloths and dish towels for the next day.

060 START FRESH

The kitchen is clean from the night before, so it's quick work to clean up after breakfast.

EMPTY Unload the dishwasher, which you filled and ran last night. In this routine, you'll never again wonder if dishes are clean or dirty.

LOAD Put breakfast dishes into the dishwasher. It only takes an extra minute or two!

WIPE Spray counters and the breakfast table with the All-Purpose Cleaner (see item 104) and then wipe clean.

RINSE Use the spray nozzle to rinse the sink. Sprinkle some baking soda, work it in with a sponge, let it sit for a few minutes, then rinse again.

SWEEP Get those breakfast crumbs!

Quick Tip

GET ALL HANDS ON DECK

Kitchen clean up is so easy and quick that it's a great opportunity to get children involved in household upkeep. Make sure the kids use non-toxic cleaners.

061
RESET THE FRIDGE

Plan on cleaning the fridge and freezer on your grocery-shopping day, since it's more efficient to clean a near-empty fridge and freezer than one packed with supplies that you'll need to unload. Remove expired food, then quickly wipe down the shelves, walls, and drawers with the Nonabrasive Vinegar Cleaner (see item 104).

Every six months, deep clean your refrigerator. Plan to do this before a major grocery restock because you'll need to completely empty both the refrigerator and freezer. And make sure to unplug the unit or turn the power off at the electrical panel before starting!

STEP ONE Empty the refrigerator and freezer, and use the frozen foods to protect perishable items by placing them all in a cooler. Put any other items on the nearest counter, organizing them by the drawer or shelf where you plan to return them.

STEP TWO Wash shelves and let dry while you wipe the interior of the fridge. To thoroughly clean glass shelves and crisper drawers, use 1 Tbsp. dishwashing liquid to 2 c. Nonabrasive Vinegar Cleaner. Wash and replace shelf liners.

STEP THREE Soap is hard to rinse away from the interior walls of a refrigerator, so use a separate spray bottle of the Nonabrasive Vinegar solution and wipe the interior walls and door compartments. The vinegar solution will help remove lingering fridge odors as well as helping to prevent new ones.

STEP FOUR If a spot is still resistant, apply a baking soda paste and let it sit for 15 minutes, then scrub with a toothbrush. Wipe away baking soda paste and residue.

STEP FIVE Before you put everything back, clean each jar and carton with a damp cloth so you don't end up putting sticky containers back on your newly clean shelves. While you're at it, check the expiration dates and toss any expired food items, along with anything you know you'll never cook with again.

STEP SIX Finally, add a new, open box of baking soda on a middle shelf to absorb future odors.

062
FREE UP THE FREEZER

If you have a freestanding freezer, follow the steps from item 061 for cleaning the refrigerator. Unplug the unit or turn it off at the electrical panel before starting the process. Plan menus ahead and try to use as much as you can out of the freezer, so there is less frozen food to remove and store when cleaning. Empty the freezer, throwing out food that has freezer burn or has been around too long.

063
DUST THE CONDENSER

Regular cleaning of the condenser coils on the back of fridges and freezers keeps them operating at maximum efficiency, reducing power usage, and extending the life of the unit. Manufacturers recommend cleaning the coils every 3–6 months, and more often if you have any pets.

READ Refer to the manufacturer's manual to locate the condenser and fan, and review any specific warnings that may apply to your particular model.

REVEAL Use a flashlight to more easily spot any obscured patches of dust or cobwebs.

CLEAN Slide a refrigerator coil brush—a long, short-bristled tool—

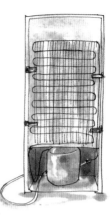

between coils to remove dust and fuzz. Work gently to avoid damage.

REMOVE Have the vacuum handy to remove dust and cobwebs from the coil brush as you work. Once finished with the refrigerator coil brush, you can vacuum the condenser with a crevice or brush attachment, again working carefully. While the unit is away from the wall, remember to vacuum the exposed floor.

064
WIPE THE EXTERIOR

There are many different types of exterior finishes available for refrigerators and freezers: enamel, regular stainless steel, fingerprint-resistant stainless steel, wooden veneer, and painted panels. Review the owner's manual for any special cleaning instructions. Cleaning these surfaces is easy to do. Simply wipe away the dirt and grime with a microfiber cloth dampened with soapy water, then rinse the cloth and wipe away any residue.

065
SHINE STAINLESS STEEL

To give stainless steel finishes a brilliant gleam, spray with the Nonabrasive Vinegar Cleaner (see item 104) and wipe clean with a microfiber cloth. To remove streaks, apply baby oil to a microfiber cloth and wipe in the direction of the grain. Flip the cloth over and wipe one more time to polish it. Keep in mind that you need to avoid abrasive cleaning products, abrasive sponges, or steel wool, as they will permanently scratch stainless steel.

Quick Tip

LINE THE FRIDGE

Each time I do a seasonal cleaning, I finish by putting washable liners on all the shelves and in the drawers. When messes happen, simply take out the liner and wash it in the sink instead of removing an entire shelf or drawer.

066

CLEAN THE OVEN

If you have a self-cleaning oven, you can use that feature according to your oven's instructions. However, you will still want to clean the oven racks separately, as described below, because the very high temperature required for a self-cleaning oven can damage the racks. I prefer using nontoxic products that I mix myself. As with all of your appliances, refer to the owner's manual for any specific dos and don'ts.

SOAK Remove the oven racks and then lay them on a towel in the bathtub, so that the racks don't damage the tub's porcelain finish. Fill the tub with 6–8 inches of hot water and add ½ c. castile soap. Soak racks overnight and then rinse thoroughly.

WIPE With the racks removed, give the oven a wipedown inside with a damp cloth in order to remove any loose crumbs.

MIX Make a paste out of baking soda and water (about 1 c. baking soda to 6 Tbsp. water).

COAT If your oven has removable heating elements, take them out. Next, cover the entire oven—including the window—with the paste and let it sit in the cold oven for at least six hours. Avoid getting any paste on the electric elements when applying it to the interior.

CLEAN Spread old towels on the floor in front of the oven to catch stray gunk. Using a moist sponge, wipe off the paste. Rinse the sponge often in clean water and continue to wipe up all vestiges of the baking soda paste. Keep a bucket of water nearby for convenient rinsing but be sure to change the water often to keep the sponge clean. Spray any resistant patches of hardened spills with white vinegar, which will help dislodge them.

067

GET A FRESH, CLEAN MICROWAVE

A boiling cup of lemon water will steam clean your microwave oven's interior. Here's how to get the best effect—and a lemony fresh scent.

WIPE Do a quick clean out of the microwave with a damp cloth and the Nonabrasive Vinegar Cleaner (see item 104). Pick up loose crumbs and anything that will come up without effort.

MIX Slice a lemon in halves, and squeeze the juice from the lemon into a microwave-safe bowl. Add

1 c. water, and add the lemon halves into the bowl as well.

BOIL Heat the bowl of lemon halves, juice, and water in the microwave for 3–5 minutes (depending on how dirty your microwave is). When the time is up, do not open the door. Let it sit for about 5 minutes more in order to steam and loosen grime inside the microwave.

FINISH Carefully remove the hot bowl and set it aside. Wipe the steamed microwave interior again. If there's a turntable or a tray, remove and wipe it as well. Go after stubborn spots with the lemon water and a cloth, and then use the lemon water as a cleaning solution on the front of the microwave door and the keypad.

Quick Tip

WIPE UP SPILLS QUICKLY

When a blueberry cobbler overflows or the roasted chicken drips coming out of the oven, it is easier to wipe up the spill while it's still warm. Do wait for the oven to cool a bit so you don't burn yourself, but if possible, get to the spill before it cools and hardens.

Want to avoid splashes and stains from cooking? Install a splash guard for easy cleanup!

068
MAINTAIN THE COOKTOP

Wiping the surface of the stove every evening takes no time at all.

Even when a pot boils over or a sauce splashes, taking care of it right away makes it easier to clean. Waiting around just makes those splashes harder to clean up, especially if they accumulate. A daily cleaning of the surface also allows you to go longer between more thorough cleanups. By design, some cooktops are easier to clean, with sealed burners that help to prevent food falling into unreachable gaps, and grates that can safely go into the dishwasher. (Remember that when you're shopping for a new one.) Whether your stovetop or cooktop needs a thorough cleaning weekly or monthly will vary with its design and use.

069   KEEP IT SIMPLE

Induction cooktops are the easiest to maintain, particularly if you wipe the smooth top right away with a damp microfiber cloth every time you cook. Any food left on the surface after cooking will soon harden from residual heat and can be tough to remove. The ceramic-glass surface is vulnerable to scratches, so avoid using any abrasive sponges or products to clean this cooktop.

To deal with hardened food, pour a little olive oil on the area to loosen the stain, then scrape with a ceramic-cooktop scraper or a paint scraper from the hardware store (hold it at a 40–45 degree angle to avoid scratching the glass). Wipe once with soapy water and then rinse with a clean sponge. If food still remains, apply a baking soda paste and let it sit for 10 minutes. Wipe again with soapy water and rinse well to remove all the baking soda paste.

070
MAKE ELECTRIC STOVES SPARKLE

Cleaning an electric stovetop is similar to a gas one in several ways—you'll wipe the surface down the same, and you will be using the same techniques to clean the knobs and control panel (see item 071). However, the electric coils require special care.

First, unplug the electric coils, which is often as simple as lifting them up and pulling out. If they're dirty, you can put a little soapy water on a microfiber cloth and rub them clean. Never submerge the coils in water. Be careful to keep the electrical connection from getting wet.

With the coils off, lift the drip pans and soak them in hot, soapy water. If they are particularly dirty, make a paste of baking soda and water (½ c. baking soda and 3 Tbsp. water) and wipe it on the drip pans, letting it sit for 30 minutes. Then scrub the burner pan with a non-abrasive sponge.

Once the coils and pans are clean, thoroughly dry them off—especially the coils—before reinstalling them.

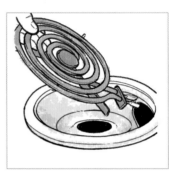

071

CARE FOR GAS STOVES

Gas stoves require a little more effort to keep clean and function at their best. Before you begin, turn on the stove and note if any of the burner holes appear to be clogged (you'll be able to tell because the flames will be uneven). Turn off the burners and let them cool completely before you start cleaning.

CLEAN GRATES & BURNER CAPS Remove the grates and the burner caps and soak them in hot soapy water for 30 minutes to an hour, while you're cleaning the rest of the stove. After soaking, use a toothbrush to scrub any cooked-on spots.

WIPE THE SURFACE Spray the top of the stove with the Nonabrasive

Vinegar Cleaner (see item 104) and wipe with a nonabrasive sponge or microfiber cloth. Add 1 Tbsp. mild soap to the vinegar solution and scrub with a toothbrush if the spot is stubborn. Then spray with clean water and wipe it off using a dry cloth.

CLEAR THE CRUMBS Gas ranges often include a way to remove crumbs and crud that have fallen below the burner units. With the grates removed, you may be able to lift the top (like the hood of a car) to clean below. There may also be a tray that pulls out from your range. In either case, take advantage of its easy access and periodically clean it.

CLEAN KNOBS Remove the knobs and wipe with the Nonabrasive Vinegar Cleaner and a microfiber cloth. Before replacing the knobs, remember to clean the control panel itself. Thoroughly dry the grates and burner caps, then return them back to their proper place.

HANDLE BURNER HEADS Remove the burner heads, which diffuse the flow of gas through holes in their exterior rim. The best way to spot a clogged hole is when the gas is lit. You don't want to handle a hot burner head, so test and note the flames an hour or so ahead. It's common for a white, powdery buildup to collect around the dispersal holes. This can be easily cleared with a pin, or paper clip. If heavier cleaning is needed, soak the heads in hot soapy water for 30 minutes. It's critical that they dry completely in a low oven for 30 minutes before replacing! (This is a good time to consult the owner's manual as the head will sit level and operate only in the right position.)

072

DON'T FORGET THE VENT HOOD

The overhead vent above your cooktop absorbs grease and smoke every time it's turned on, which means that its filters need a good cleaning every 3–6 months. You can clean the filters on the low-heat cycle of your dishwasher, but they usually have so much collected grease that it's best to wash them without other dishes in the cycle. If you wash them by hand, a long soak is recommended.

STEP ONE Spray an appropriate cleaning solution on the surface panels

of the vent hood. Depending on the surface material, choose either the Nonabrasive Vinegar Cleaner (see item 104), a mild soap solution, or follow guidelines for stainless steel (see item 065). Wipe clean with a microfiber cloth. If you have not done

this in a while, ready yourself for the collected grime and resolve to clean the hood more often!

STEP TWO Remove the filters and put them in the sink or someplace large enough to submerge them in water. Sprinkle ½ c. baking soda on top of the filters and fill the sink or tub with scalding water (from the tap or boiled in a kettle). Let the filters soak for a few minutes to help break up any caked-on grease. After soaking, scrub lightly and persistently with a soft-bristled brush that will not damage the delicate filters in the hood.

STEP THREE Rinse with water and let the filters air-dry. Put them back in the vent hood after they have completely dried out.

073

WASH BY HAND

Proclamations on what should and should not be washed in a dishwasher are a surefire way to start an argument between the closest of friends. The truth is that all dishwashers are not created equal, so what works for you may not work for others. Below are items that I think should always be washed by hand to avoid even a chance of damage, or will be worth a few minutes of extra effort.

MATERIAL	WASHING DIRECTIONS
FINE CHINA AND CRYSTAL	They are delicate and deserve to be treated as such. Gilded edges absolutely should not be in the dishwasher where they will darken and discolor. I like to wash them by hand with my husband after all the guests have gone home while catching up on the details of the event.
WOODEN COOKING UTENSILS AND CUTTING BOARDS	Rinse them by hand and apply baking soda to eliminate stains from beets, strawberries, cherries, and other foods.
KITCHEN KNIVES	The heat and detergent will dull knife blades and may loosen the handles. Better to wipe them clean and dry them after use, immediately storing them in a knife slot where the blade is protected.
SILVERWARE	Attitudes about putting silverware in the dishwasher have relaxed over time. It's up to you how careful you want to be with your silverware. Hand-wash if that ritual is important to you. It's okay to put silverware in the dishwasher but make certain that none of your everyday stainless flatware comes in contact. The stainless will scratch and discolor the softer silver.
PLASTIC UTENSILS AND STORAGE CONTAINERS	I prefer to hand-wash mine but washing on the top shelf of the dishwasher is usually safe for most plastics.
SILVER SERVICE PIECES	Silver service dishes risk getting beat up in the dishwasher so wash them by hand in hot, sudsy water as soon as guests leave and dry with a soft towel. Foods with salt, mayonnaise, and eggs will discolor silver if left to dry, and soaking in water overnight will also damage the silver. Give them immediate attention!
CAST-IRON SKILLETS AND POTS	Sprinkle a generous cover of salt on the interior surface and rub it in with a plastic scrubber. The salt absorbs grease and food without water that will rust cast iron. It's okay to then lightly rinse with warm water but thoroughly dry to avoid rusting. If you rinse with water, apply a thin coat of vegetable oil and wipe with a paper towel to protect the seasoned finish before storing.
NONSTICK COOKWARE	Manufacturers recommend whether or not to put their nonstick pans in the dishwasher, but if you're particular about their care, wash them by hand.
COPPER POTS AND PANS	Copper will lose its luster in the dishwasher. Instead, hand-wash in warm, soapy water. If food is baked on, soak the pan in water until the food loosens. Avoid scrubbing!
EVERYDAY POTS AND PANS	Assuming you've been filling the dishwasher since breakfast, there may not be a lot of room left. Pots and pans, even if they are dishwasher safe, take up a lot of space and crusted food doesn't always get effectively cleaned in the dishwasher. Take a few minutes to hand-wash them.

074
WASH MORE EFFICIENTLY

Although there's not really a wrong way to wash dishes by hand, there may be a better way than your current system. Increasing your efficiency will save time and energy better spent on other things.

SOAK Fill your sink or a large rubber basin with hot, sudsy water and let your dishes soak for a few minutes. A little bit of soaking can help loosen stuck-on food, especially greasy residues and dried-up food particles.

SELECT Choose a type of item to wash and tackle the entire group, rather than randomly selecting items. Whether you start with dishes, bowls, cups, or flatware, similar items will fit more efficiently on your dish rack.

WASH Scrub the food off your dishes in the soapy water, so the water can help separate loosened food from the dishes. Use the hottest water your hands can handle.

RINSE When finished—or at least finished with a batch that fills your basin—dump the dirty water and start rinsing the dishes with the rinse water collecting in the basin. If all the dishes are washed and in the basin, the collecting rinse water will further help dislodge the food you loosened with the wash sponge. If you have another batch to do, add dish soap to the collected rinse water to continue the process.

DRY Allow your dishes to sit, even for a minute, so excess water can drip into the dish drain instead of prematurely saturating your dishtowel.

REPLACE Another benefit of washing in item groups is how you can efficiently put them away in one place, rather than having to move back and forth to different cabinets and drawers.

075
CLEAN THE DISHWASHER

You depend on your dishwasher to do the workhorse job of cleaning your dirty dishes, glasses, flatware, casseroles, and pots. But it will need regular cleaning itself, too. Have a look at these various items, and remember these easy steps to insure that every load of dishes comes out sparkling clean from a pristine dishwasher.

076
WIPE THE EXTERIOR

Daily, if necessary, wipe around the controls and handle of your dishwasher. If you have a wooden or painted decorative panel on the front, use a barely dampened cloth to wipe it down.

For stainless steel, clean with a microfiber cloth and the Nonabrasive Vinegar Cleaner (see item 104). Next, apply baby oil to a microfiber cloth and wipe in the direction of the grain. Flip the cloth over and wipe one more time to finish polishing it.

077
LEARN TO LOAD

Modern dishwashers are engineered to do a superior job of cleaning and sanitizing compared to washing by hand, and with less wasted water. If dinnerware isn't coming out clean and you've given the machine a deep cleanse (see item 079), it could be human error in loading the dishwasher.

How you place your things in the dishwasher can make a difference in how clean they get: Position each piece so that water can reach it, and avoid overcrowding that may chip, break, or scratch when jostling in the cycle.

078
BANISH ODORS

Once a month, pour 1 c. white vinegar into the bottom of the empty dishwasher and set it to run through a heavy wash cycle. Vinegar cuts grease, deodorizes, and sanitizes.

For extra freshening power, sprinkle 1 c. baking soda in the bottom of the dishwasher and run through a second, light cycle.

079
DEEP CLEAN

Every 6 months, the dishwasher and filter need a serious cleaning. Repeat the process more often if dishes and glasses just don't appear as clean as you like them—you may even save yourself the cost of a repairman's visit. Although soaking may extend the total time, your active time should be less than an hour.

STEP ONE Remove the racks and the flatware bin.

STEP TWO Remove the filter. Most are easy to remove but consult the owner's manual if you're uncertain how to get it off. Clean with soapy water, and scrub with a toothbrush if food is caught in the mesh cover.

STEP THREE Fill the sink with water and add 2 c. vinegar. Put the filter and the racks into the water and soak for at least an hour and as long as overnight. For racks too big to fit in the sink, soak them in the bathtub.

STEP FOUR Clear holes in the spinning arm that appear to be blocked. Use a toothpick or fine wire to open each hole, working carefully.

STEP FIVE Dampen a cloth with a solution of equal parts vinegar and water, and wipe the interior surfaces before putting the filter, racks, and flatware bin back in.

080
MIND THE FLOW

Whether you're cleaning on the top or bottom rack, place the dirty side toward the center and down, facing the rotating arms that circulate the water. Pay attention to anything that might block the water flow. For instance, tall dinner plates, trays, and large casserole dishes should go on the outer edges of the rack. After loading, spin the arm to make certain nothing is blocking it. And don't put anything toward the front that would block the detergent dispenser!

Plates and bowls that are vertically stacked will need space between them so the water can get to their surfaces. The racks that have vertical tines are designed to leave space around items as long as you don't overcrowd the dishes as you load them. The upper rack is often more open for free-form loading of small bowls, cups, and glasses.

Don't let pieces touch, which can restrict adequate water flow and risk breakage from vibrations during the wash cycle. Set cups and mugs at an angle so that their handles don't protrude. Overloading the washer might seem like you're saving time and water, but you could end up having to rewash any pieces that didn't get clean the first time around.

081
TRUST THE POWER

It isn't necessary to pre-rinse dishes in the sink, but you should scrape leftover food off that may clog the drain to the disposal. Also remove proteins, such as eggs and cheese, right away since they can harden on the plate as they sit.

PACK YOUR BASKET Manufacturers recommend loading flatware with the handles down for the most efficient cleaning. The exceptions are meat forks, knives, and any sharp utensil, which should be placed with the sharp end down to avoid accidental cuts. Make sure spoons and forks do not nest inside one another and block water from reaching them. Most baskets have an optional slotted screen that will hold the pieces away from each other during the wash cycle. When you've got a lot of flatware to load, put the screen in place first and fit individual pieces in through the slots.

USE ALL CYCLES Make use of the various settings to boost cleaning, conserve energy, and tailor the cycle to the load. If you don't yet have a full load, run a rinse cycle rather than letting food harden on the dishes.

082

KNOW
YOUR SINK

Much like carpets and countertops, your sink's composition dictates the best course of action for cleaning. Its properties also present unique vulnerabilities, so use the suggested cleaning-solution recipes in this book.

MATERIAL	DAILY	TIPS & TRICKS	AVOID
STAINLESS STEEL	Rinse, then sprinkle with baking soda. Spray with the Nonabrasive Vinegar Cleaner (see item 104), scrub with a sponge, then rinse again. Avoid water spots by drying the sink with a towel.	Occasionally wipe the sink with a little olive oil on a cloth to restore its shine.	Ammonia and bleach, as well as any abrasive cleaners and rough scrubbing pads.
PORCELAIN ENAMEL OVER CAST IRON	Clean after each use with mild dishwashing liquid and hot water. Rinse and dry.	Sprinkle baking soda on stains, and scrub with the cut-side of a lemon. Rinse and dry.	Immediately remove tea bags, coffee, blueberries, red wine, mayonnaise, mustard, and pickles, or risk taking on permanent stains.
FIRECLAY	Clean with the Nonabrasive Vinegar Cleaner. Dry with a towel to prevent water spots.	Sprinkle baking soda on resistant stains. Scrub with a soft sponge. Rinse and dry.	Harsh scouring powders and commercial drain cleaners.
SOLID SURFACE	Clean with warm, soapy water and a sponge, then rinse and dry. Treat with the Disinfectant (see item 104) after raw meat or poultry has been in the sink.	Use a non-scratching scrubber with baking soda or vinegar to get rid of stains.	Water that dries on the surface creates an unsightly film, so dry often. And remember, hot pots and pans can scorch.
COMPOSITE GRANITE AND COMPOSITE QUARTZ	Use only mild soap (pH neutral) and a soft cloth. Rinse well and dry with a towel after every use.	Reseal the sinks annually to minimize staining.	Food stains and hard water can permanently etch the surface. Citrus, vinegar, and ammonia can strip the finish.
ACRYLIC COMPOSITE	Use mild soap and water, and always rinse well. Dry with a towel after each use to avoid water spotting.	On stains only, step up to the Nonabrasive Vinegar Cleaner.	Abrasives will scratch the surface, and hot pots will scorch.
SOAPSTONE	Scrub with a mild soap and sponge to diminish the white haze that often develops with hard water. Rinse well to remove soap, and dry.	Every 4–6 weeks, rub olive oil into the stone. Let it absorb for 30 minutes to an hour, then buff dry.	Abrasives will scratch the surface, and lemon juice and vinegar will etch the stone.
COPPER	Wash with mild soap and a sponge. Rinse well, and dry off the metal using a microfiber cloth.	Most new copper sinks have an applied patina that will be damaged by abrasive scrubbing.	Acidic foods (citrus, tomatoes, and vinegar) will pit the surface. Abrasive scrubbers will scratch.

083
RECHARGE THE DISPOSAL

A garbage disposal takes only a little care to operate efficiently, banishing smells and keeping the drains clear.

FRESHEN WITH CITRUS Anytime you cook or eat a lemon or orange, drop in a few peels when you run the disposal. Once a week, put a wedge or a Garbage Disposal Bomb (see item 104) into the disposal, and run it with cold water for a few seconds to clean the blades and freshen the space.

084
MAINTAIN YOUR DISPOSAL

Always run cold water before, during, and after the disposal is switched on and off. This serves three purposes: It helps shift food around inside the disposal to maximize the chances it will get chopped up; flowing water will help push the food particles through your pipes, decreasing the chance of clogs; and cold water solidifies any foodstuff that liquefies when hot, such as oil and cheese. It's better to have small, solid chunks go through your disposal than liquids that may cool into a coating, or solidify into a blockage down the line.

DEEP CLEAN Every two weeks put ½ c. baking soda down the disposal. Chase it with 1 c. vinegar. It will fizz just like a middle school science project, killing some bacteria in the disposal and drain. But more importantly, the minute bubbling will help dislodge bits of food and muck that have gotten caught in this dangerous and hard-to-reach place. Leave it for 10 minutes before pouring a kettle full of boiling water down the drain.

ICE IT DOWN During spring and fall, dump a tray full of ice cubes down the disposal, follow with a cup of rock salt, then turn on the cold water and the disposal. The whirling blades of the disposal will turn the ice and rock salt into a blizzard of shrapnel, scouring the walls that you can't reach while also cleaning the blades.

Never put chemicals such as bleach or drain cleaners in the disposal. They can damage the blades, rubber and plastic parts, and the plumbing.

Don't overload a disposal. Give it time to process and clear smaller handfuls before adding more.

If a clog occurs, unplug the disposal or turn it off at the electrical panel. Never try to unclog it while it's attached to its power source, even if no one else is around to accidentally turn on the activation switch.

If it stops while still partially filled, use kitchen tongs to remove the food. If fibrous strings or a stray rubber band gets wrapped around the blades, remove them with needle-nose pliers. Be very careful when putting any tools in the cavity.

085
KEEP IT CLEAR

Some foods should never be put into a disposal because they risk either clogging the drains or damaging the disposal's mechanics. The list below should go into the compost or trash.

TRASH

Grease and Fat Pour bacon grease, oil discarded after frying or sautéing, and other fats into empty bottles with caps; toss when the bottle is full.

Bones They'll dull the disposal blades and clog the plumbing, and shards could be propelled out of the hole.

Pasta and Rice With exposure to water in the disposal, they will expand and solidify in the pipes beyond the disposal, resulting in a glob that won't allow water through.

COMPOST

Eggshells They don't completely break down in the disposal and can clog plumbing.

Fruit Pits and Seeds Hard pits and even small seeds are just too hard for the small blades of a disposal.

Celery, Kale, Rhubarb Tough, fibrous foods can get wrapped around the disposal blades, inhibiting their movement.

Potato and Carrot Peels Whenever there are a lot of vegetable peels, they clump into a paste, making it hard for the disposal to keep up with the volume and risking a clog or shutdown.

Onion and Garlic Skins Bulb skins are too thin to break down in the blades, and often cling to the walls of the disposal.

086
CARE FOR FAUCETS

A quick, daily towel wipe will keep your sink hardware looking like new. Most kitchen faucets, handles, and other built-in sink accessories installed within the last twenty years have a factory-applied coating that is stain and tarnish resistant. You only need to wipe the hardware with a soft cloth after every use to remove fingerprints and water spotting. Be diligent because minerals in the water and soap scum that are left to sit will wear away the protective coating over time.

PROTECT THE COATING Your goal is to preserve the faucet's protective coating because if the coating is scratched or chipped, the base material is exposed to oxidization and can discolor. Stay away from abrasive cleaners and cleaning pads, bleach, ammonia, rubbing alcohol, acidic solutions, cleaning products designed to remove tarnish or rust, and polishes with harsh chemicals. Multiple

manufacturers use an incredibly thin physical vapor deposition process or clean protective coated finishes on fixtures of brass, copper, bronze, stainless, chrome or nickel, so it may be impossible to identify whether an existing fixture is coated or not.

PLAY IT SAFE If you can identify the manufacturer, check their website for specific cleaning instructions. If you're cleaning blind and want to remove accumulated water spots or soap, start with warm soapy water, rinse well to remove all traces of soap, dry, and buff with a microfiber cloth. A soft toothbrush can get at dirt that may build at the joints.

087
ENJOY LIVING FINISHES

Uncoated brass, copper, and bronze are known as "living" finishes which beautifully change over time. These are prized for the patina they develop with age and wear; just keep water spots and soap scum off of them.

088
CLEAN OLDER FAUCETS RIGHT

Older, uncoated fixtures can be scratched by abrasive scrubbers, so only use soft cloths and sponges. Try these steps to maintain vintage faucets and knobs.

STEP ONE Start with soapy water, wiping with a soft cloth, rinse well, dry, and buff.

STEP TWO Step up to the Nonabrasive Vinegar Cleaner (see item 104), wiping with a microfiber cloth.

STEP THREE Baking soda is a mild abrasive and is the next possibility. Sprinkle baking soda and let it sit for 5 minutes, rinse well, dry, and buff. Repeat this step if you're beginning to see results.

STEP FOUR For really grungy fixtures, use the Nonabrasive Vinegar Cleaner to make a baking soda paste and apply for 5 minutes. Rinse, dry, and buff.

089
CLEAN SEALED COUNTERTOPS

Stone countertops have a beautiful mix of colors and patterns—the natural swirls of marble, the magnificent speckling of granite, the subtle color shades and embedded fossils of limestone, and the randomness of cured concrete are all visually interesting. But that beauty comes at a cost: the porous nature of these stones make them extremely vulnerable to stains. They must be resealed annually to retain a semblance of stain resistance. But even sealed, these countertops are delicate and can be damaged, so keep these care tips in mind.

AVOID Acidic foods like citrus, tomatoes, red and white wine, tea, and coffee can compromise the sealant and chemically etch the surface. Abrasive cleaners, hot pans, and vinegar-based solutions can also damage the surface.

WASH Water with a little dish soap and a microfiber cloth are all you need for daily cleaning, but remember to dry with a clean cloth to avoid water spots.

APPLY If a stain does appear, rub in a paste of baking soda and water, cover with plastic wrap, seal the edges with tape, and leave in place for 24 hours—the baking-soda paste will help draw out the stain. After the sitting period, wipe with soapy water, rinse with clean water, and dry well.

RESEAL Most penetrating sealants are simple to use. They usually need a thorough cleaning before applying the sealant, as well as time for the sealant to seep into the surface. Make sure to check instructions to ensure proper protection.

090
SAVE UNSEALED COUNTERTOPS

BAMBOO Give this surface a daily dusting followed by a wipe with a damp cloth. For deeper cleaning, start with soapy water. Stains can be treated with a thick salt paste and rubbed with a nonabrasive sponge. Rinse well and repeat as necessary.

BUTCHER BLOCK Wipe with the Nonabrasive Vinegar Cleaner—be sure not to saturate and risk warping—and dry with a microfiber cloth. For fresh stains, sprinkle some salt on the stain and scrub with the cut side of a lemon half, let rest for a few minutes, then lightly rinse with water and dry. A food-safe oil applied every six months will help protect porous butcher block.

CERAMIC TILE Acid-based cleaners and aggressive scrubbing can dull a tile's glossy finish. Simply wipe with soapy water and microfiber cloth, dry, and buff with a dry towel to preserve the shine. Sanitize the grout once a week by spraying with the Disinfectant (see item 104), letting it sit for a few minutes, then scrubbing with a grout brush or toothbrush. Rinse with hot water and dry with a microfiber cloth.

COMPOSITE QUARTZ Don't let spills dry; a damp microfiber cloth will do the trick, followed by a rinse with clean water and drying to avoid water spots. If food does dry on quartz, carefully scrape it away with the bowl of a plastic spoon and wipe with a nonabrasive sponge, soap, and water.

LAMINATE Wipe with soapy water and a microfiber cloth for cleaning daily, or a little baking soda and water on a soft-bristle brush for a deep clean.

LAVA STONE Clean this surface with the All-Purpose Cleaner (see item 104) and a microfiber cloth, and spray with the Disinfectant weekly.

PAPER Countertops made from recycled paper are available in a range of sealed and unsealed finishes that necessitate different deep-cleaning methods. Start with a daily wash with soapy water, and consult the directions for your specific type of finish to determine how to tackle stains.

RECYCLED GLASS Wipe with soapy water, and immediately remove any acidic foods like citrus if the glass is suspended in acrylic. For glass in a cement binder, follow the directions in item 089.

SLATE AND SOAPSTONE These non-porous stones just need wiping with soapy water and a rinse.

SOLID SURFACE Also known as Corian and other brand-specific names, solid surfaces just need a little soapy water for most messes. Rub a baking-soda paste on tough stains, rinse and wipe dry.

STAINLESS STEEL Spray with the Nonabrasive Vinegar Cleaner (see item 104) and wipe with a microfiber cloth with the grain. Abrasive sponges and cleaners will scratch the surface. For stains, gently rub a baking-soda paste with the grain, then rinse and dry with a microfiber cloth.

Be careful—hot pots and pans can scorch many countertops, and dropping them can chip and scratch surfaces.

Cutting boards protect your kitchen countertops from stains, cuts, and scratches.

091 WASH BOARDS

Cutting boards protect your counters from cuts, but they are even more essential for protecting your family from food-borne illnesses. A good rule of thumb is to use two cutting boards: a wooden one for fruit, vegetables, and bread, and a plastic cutting board for meat.

Never cut raw meat on a wooden board, because bacteria can leach into the wood, leading to cross-contamination of the next thing you cut on the same board.

HAND-WASH THE WOOD Dishwashers generate heat and steam that can warp and split wood, so always hand-wash them. Scrub a wooden board with a stiff brush and soapy water, then spray it with the Nonabrasive Vinegar Cleaner (see item 104) and let it sit a few minutes.

Vinegar goes a long way toward killing household germs, bacteria, mold, and mildew. Rinse well with water and let it air-dry. Make sure it's completely dry because any moisture will encourage the growth of bacteria.

PUT PLASTIC IN THE DISHWASHER Plastic cutting boards benefit from a run through the dishwasher because of its high heat and strong detergent. First, rinse and scrub the board to dispose of any bits of food and bacteria. These boards are very easy to clean, but they also become compromised with general use and knife marks that create openings for bacteria. You should replace them every few years. You may need to retrieve your plastic cutting board from the dishwasher before the drying cycle as it may warp with heat. Check the care instructions when purchasing.

092 REFRESH THE COFFEE MAKER

Despite the fact that boiling water and abrasive coffee grounds are part of every cup of coffee, the coffee maker still needs a good scrub—it can grow more mold and bacteria than you want to imagine. So don't imagine it. Just clean it monthly for peace of mind and better tasting coffee! Here's how to clean a standard drip machine. (For instructions on your restaurant-grade espresso machine or Keurig, consult the owner's manual.)

STEP ONE Rinse the carafe and permanent filter with warm soapy water. Spray the exterior of the machine with the Non-Abrasive Vinegar cleaner (see item 104) and wipe off old stains.

STEP TWO Mix equal parts vinegar and water in the carafe and pour into the water dispenser. Put a paper filter or permanent filter in place to catch any debris, and start the brew cycle.

STEP THREE Halfway through the cycle, turn it off for an hour, then turn it back on to finish the brew cycle.

STEP FOUR Rinse the carafe and fill the water dispenser with plain water. Start another brew cycle. If you still smell vinegar, run a third cycle with more clean water.

093 CLEAN YOUR KNIFE BLOCK

You clean your knives every time you use them. What about the knife block? Dust and crumbs accumulate in its slots. Periodically turn the vacuum on high suction and hold it over the slots. Clean the exterior as you would a wood cutting board (see item 091).

094 TEND TO A TOASTER OVEN

Cleaning a toaster oven is pretty straightforward. Unplug it and take out all racks and trays (particularly the crumb tray on the bottom). Dump any loose debris and soak them in hot soapy water. Spray the interior and exterior with the Nonabrasive Vinegar Cleaner (see item 104) and wipe with a damp cloth.

Quick Tip

SPRAY THE PRODUCE

Naturally clean your fruits and veggies with a nontoxic produce spray. Combine 1 c. water to 1 c. distilled white vinegar in a spray bottle. Add 10 drops of lemon essential oil and mix well. Spray your produce before cooling eating, then rinse.

095 PROCESS THE PROCESSOR

Cleaning the food processor is a quick task that's important to take care of every time you use it. Remove the bowl, blade, and other accessories and empty the bowl. Soak all in warm soapy water. After 10 minutes, scrub with a microfiber cloth or sponge. Spray the motor base of the machine with the Non-Abrasive Vinegar Cleaner (see item 104), and wipe with a microfiber cloth. Dry all of the elements and put the processor back together.

096 BE GOOD TO YOUR BLENDER

Basic blender maintenance is simple and satisfying. Start off by pouring very hot water into the blender jar. Then, add two squirts of dishwashing liquid, put the lid on, and blend for 10 to 15 seconds. Pour out the dirty water, rinse it well, and dry.

DEEP CLEAN If you use your blender for daily smoothies or pureed soups, you should take it apart once a week and soak the removable rubber gasket and the blade. Give the rest of the blender base a quick spray of the Nonabrasive Vinegar Cleaner (see item 104) and wipe clean with a microfiber cloth.

097 HANDLE HIGH-PERFORMANCE BLENDERS

A new generation of more powerful blenders has surfaced with the desire for health-conscious smoothies. It takes a motor with higher horsepower to shear kale and other tough produce into a drinkable liquid, and these motors are designed to last a lifetime. Clean the containers and accessories well so they will last a lifetime, too.

Refer to your owner's manual before cleaning for the first time. Some containers, lids, and blades can go on the top rack of the dishwasher, but manufacturers may advise against putting any part in the dishwasher.

DAILY Leaving food to dry in the blender can damage the blades and the container, but a quick clean after each use is easy. Rinse the container in warm—not hot—water. Fill the blender jar no more than halfway with water and add only a drop or two of dishwashing soap. Let it run for 30–60 seconds; rinse again and air-dry.

MONTHLY Every month or two, fill half the jar with vinegar and add enough water to reach the top. Let that soak for half a day. Rinse and repeat cleaning with soapy water as described above.

DEEP CLEAN If your blender sees everyday use, you may begin to see a cloudy film inside the container. Minerals from fruits and vegetables are to blame, but you can get rid of the film. Pour 1 c. white vinegar into

098 JUICE IT

Electric juicers are designed for easy cleaning, but the following steps should be taken every time they're used.

STEP ONE Unplug the machine and disassemble all removable parts.

STEP TWO Empty the pulp and seeds into the compost.

STEP THREE Rinse all detachable accessories and soak them in warm, soapy water.

STEP FOUR Use a toothbrush to reach tight spots and to clean a mesh strainer. If the mesh strainer still has debris, add baking soda to the soap and water solution and let it soak for an additional 10 minutes.

STEP FIVE Rinse with clean water, air-dry, and reassemble.

the container and fill it with water, leaving it to soak for several hours to overnight. If needed, use a soft scrubber on the inside, while taking care around the sharp edges of the blades.

099
CLEAN OUT THE CABINETS

Kitchen cabinets accumulate a layer of grime from the grease and steam in everyday cooking, but a quick wipe with warm soapy water once a week will keep it from getting noticeably thick. Tackle the spills and drips when they happen. Make it a habit to do a daily spot check to look for a spill that you may have missed. Every six months, empty the cabinets and do an all-out sweep of the interior shelves where crumbs and minor spills have escaped your attention.

100
BRIGHTEN CABINET DOORS

Cabinets with natural and painted wood, laminate, and stainless steel doors need only a few minutes of your attention to keep them looking beautiful. Just remember to avoid any abrasive sponges, scrubbers or cleaning products, which will scratch and dull the finish.

STEP ONE Mist a solution of castile soap and warm water on a microfiber cloth and wipe the cabinet and drawer panels.

STEP TWO Wipe again with a clean damp cloth to remove the soap and once again with a clean dry cloth.

STEP THREE Inspect the hinges and hardware connections, and use a toothbrush to dislodge grime that you find.

Quick Tip

STERILIZE YOUR SPONGE

Your sponge may get so dirty that rinsing is not enough. Add it to the top rack of your dishwasher for your next load. You can squeeze out excess water and microwave it for four minutes, and the heat will kill most of the bacteria.

101
CLEAN BEHIND CLOSED DOORS

Hidden spaces on the inside of cabinets, drawers, and the pantry can often get overlooked in between cooking and family life. The worst cases are often the junk drawer and the space under the sink, but all interior spaces need a seasonal cleaning to avoid crud creep. There's no better time to declutter, tossing seldom-used utensils, matchbooks, and overflowing rubber bands. If you just can't part with the special occasion utensils or little-used pots and pans, move them to a shelf or drawer on the edge of your work area.

EXPOSE Throw open all the doors and cabinets and empty them—grouping the contents in the order you intend to restore them—and stash them in bins.

CLEANSE Take the time to thoroughly vacuum all interior spaces with the dust-brush attachment, then wipe with a soft cloth or sponge dampened with the All-Purpose Cleaner (see item 104).

EXCAVATE Scrub the edges and cracks with a toothbrush before wiping away the cleaner with a cloth dampened with water only.

SHINE While they're out, wipe all utensils with the Nonabrasive Vinegar Cleaner (see item 104).

REPLACE Let drawers and shelves dry completely before returning the contents. Use the same process to clean pantry shelves.

102
DON'T LET SPILLS LINGER

It's important to keep the shelves of your cabinets clean, otherwise an unattended mess will transfer to every jar, box, can, and bottle that you store. Oftentimes, the type of spill will determine the best course of action.

GREASY Use the Nonabrasive Vinegar Solution (see item 104). Vinegar cuts through grease, making it easy to remove with a microfiber cloth. You may need to make two passes, as your first wiping may lift off most of the loosened grease but spread the remainder.

STICKY For peanut butter or honey drips, fill a plastic bag with ice and hold it on the spill until it hardens. Then gently scrape it off with the bowl of a plastic spoon.

COLORFUL If there are spots of juice or wine stains that don't come off, generously sprinkle baking soda on a barely damp sponge and hold it over the spot, repeating as needed. Rinse to remove all traces of baking soda and dry the spot.

103
GET A HANDLE ON IT

Cabinet and drawer handles are the primary point of human contact, so they're continually exposed to the dirt and oils of your hands. They're also easy to overlook, since it's specifically the inside of a door pull or knob that's handled.

Wash knobs and handles with hot soapy water and a soft cloth; then dry and buff with another cloth. During the winter months when colds spread through the family, spray them with the Disinfectant (see item 104) to decrease the chance of lingering germs.

104 MIX IT IN THE KITCHEN

Keep your kitchen looking—and smelling—fantastic with these simple, natural recipes to create homemade cleaning supplies.

ALL-PURPOSE CLEANER
2 tsp. borax, ¼ tsp. liquid castile soap, 10 drops lemon essential oil.

Mix all ingredients with hot water in a 16-oz. spray bottle.

DISINFECTANT 2 Tbsp. liquid castile soap, 20 drops tea tree oil.

Mix the soap and essential oil with hot water in a 16-oz. spray bottle.

GARBAGE DISPOSAL BOMBS
(makes 24 bombs) ½ c. citric acid, 1½ c. baking soda, 30 drops orange essential oil.

Mix all ingredients in a bowl until thoroughly combined. Use a spray bottle to mist just enough water for the mixture to hold its shape. Mold the mixture into small balls with a rounded tablespoon and place on a cookie sheet to dry overnight. Store in an airtight container.

NONABRASIVE VINEGAR CLEANER
1 part white vinegar, 2 parts water, 5 drops lavender essential oil.

Combine the vinegar and water in a 16-oz. spray bottle. Add 5 drops of essential oils if you don't like the smell of vinegar—my favorites are lavender, grapefruit, orange, lemon, and peppermint.

KITCHEN
Checklists

The challenge of thinking, "I'll just wash this dish later," is how that one dish quickly turns into two dishes. . . and four bowls, and three drinking glasses, and a scattering of utensils! Take care of those dirty dishes, stovetop drips, and other small cleanups before they become snowball into bigger messes.

Numbers refer to the general cleaning entries, so make sure to reference the appropriate supporting items to address specific materials and circumstances.

DAILY

- ☐ Sweep or vacuum floors *30*
- ☐ Wipe counters and tables *89*
- ☐ Wipe stovetop *68*
- ☐ Wash dishes *73*
- ☐ Load and run dishwasher *77*
- ☐ Wipe dishwasher exterior *76*
- ☐ Clean sink *82*
- ☐ Wipe faucets *86*
- ☐ Clean minor appliances *92*
- ☐ Put out new dishtowels *59*

WEEKLY

- ☐ Dust window treatments *14*
- ☐ Dust doors and baseboards *18*
- ☐ Clean switch plates *19*
- ☐ Dust ceilings and walls *20*
- ☐ Mop floors *31*
- ☐ Dust lampshades and chandeliers *52, 56*
- ☐ Clean refrigerator interior/exterior *61*
- ☐ Clean stovetop *68*
- ☐ Clean disposal *83*
- ☐ Wipe cabinet doors *100*
- ☐ Disinfect handles and knobs *103*
- ☐ _____
- ☐ _____

MONTHLY

- ☐ Clean window treatments *14*
- ☐ Wash trash bins *28*
- ☐ Clean doorknobs *29*
- ☐ Steam-clean microwave *67*
- ☐ Sanitize dishwasher interior *78*
- ☐ Deep-clean disposal *83*
- ☐ Deep-clean minor appliances *92*
- ☐ Clean knobs *103*
- ☐ _____

SEASONALLY (SPRING AND FALL)

- ☐ Wash windows *12*
- ☐ Deep-clean window treatments *14*
- ☐ Wipe doors and baseboards *18*
- ☐ Clean walls *20*
- ☐ Clean light fixtures, chandeliers, and sconces *54, 56, 57*
- ☐ Deep-clean refrigerator and freezer *61*
- ☐ Replace liners *61*
- ☐ Clean condenser coils *63*
- ☐ Deep-clean stove and oven *66*
- ☐ Clean vent hood and filter *72*
- ☐ Deep-clean dishwasher and filter *79*
- ☐ Scour disposal *83*
- ☐ Clean knife block *93*
- ☐ Clean out cabinets and pantry *99*
- ☐ Clean inside cabinets and drawers *99*
- ☐ Reseal countertops *89*

Bathroom

A routine keeps bathrooms fresh and clean.

As you create a bathroom routine, teach it to your children. It's important that they learn how to clean up after themselves. And by using natural cleaning products, there's no need for you to worry about harsh chemicals. In this section, you'll learn how to conquer tough matters like mold, mildew, and water stains. You'll also learn about the different materials that make up your tub, countertops, and sinks, and what cleaning methods are best for each. I'll guide you through how to care for towels, bath mats, and odors, and I'll share cleaning tips and tricks throughout the section. And I include recommendations on how to minimize the chance of spreading colds and flus when a family member feels under the weather.

An uncluttered bathroom is not only easier to clean, it also appears cleaner without a counter jammed with bottles.

105
START THE DAY RIGHT

A clean and uncluttered bathroom gives the day an energizing kick-start. Designate a quick five minutes to the bathroom-tidying items below every evening before bed and every morning after you're ready for the day. It's cathartic, a symbolic taking control of your space that propels you through the rest of your day.

- ☐ Quickly wipe down faucets, sinks, and counters

- ☐ Swish the toilets

- ☐ Clean the shower as you finish, using a squeegee to wipe away soap scum and water minerals

- ☐ Pick up dirty clothes and put them in the hamper

Quick Tip

USE A COLOR CODE

Microfiber cloths absorb more than a soft cloth, rag, or sponge, but use a different cloth for general cleaning than for cleaning the toilet. I buy one of a different color for the toilet so I'm less likely to confuse them. I also keep a second pair of rubber gloves in the same color as the designated toilet cloth. Microfiber cloths used in the bath don't rest in the laundry hamper with clothes; they go directly into the washer in a load by themselves.

106
STOCK A BATH CADDY

If cleaners are within easy reach, you're more apt to use them daily. Store the shower cleaner on the rack with soap and shampoo. Stash other supplies beneath the sink or in nearby cabinets. If there's no extra space behind closed doors, organize supplies in a stylish wicker basket or metal caddy. If you prefer a basket, pick one with sides just higher than the tallest bottle to shield supplies.

- ☐ All-Purpose Cleaner
- ☐ Disinfectant
- ☐ Glass Cleaner
- ☐ Nonabrasive Vinegar Cleaner
- ☐ Rubber gloves for general cleaning
- ☐ Rubber gloves in another color for toilet
- ☐ Toilet Bowl Bombs
- ☐ Tub 'n' Tile Cleaner

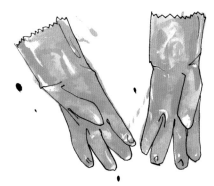

107
KEEP IT FRESH

Given damp towels, dirty clothes, and regular use, the bathroom can deliver daily olfactory assaults. Implement a few steps to keep it smelling as clean as it looks.

Turn on the vent when you enter the bath to help remove both excess moisture and bacteria in the air. Open a window whenever possible to allow the moisture to dissipate.

ABSORB Fill a cute bowl with baking soda to absorb odors.

CONTAIN Invest in a lidded wastebasket and empty it often.

FRESHEN Keep a fresh arrangement of sweet-smelling flowers in a vase or light a scented candle when you have guests in the house.

RELEASE Add a few drops of essential oil onto the side of the toilet paper roll. Each time you unroll it, the aromatherapy will be released into the air.

108
ORGANIZE YOUR MEDICINE CABINET

The bathroom medicine cabinet is one of those places that collects clutter and develops a layer of grime from humidity and dust. Follow these steps to keep it just as fresh as the rest of your bathroom.

EMPTY Pull everything out of the cabinet and throw out anything you won't use, including little foil sample packets of lotion, perfume and cologne, and beauty products. If you haven't used it in a year, you probably never will!

STERILIZE Spray the interior of the cabinet with the Disinfectant (see item 149), and wipe all shelves and crevices. If you have removable glass shelves, take them out and clean with the Glass Cleaner (see item 149).

RESTOCK Add back the things you'll actually use, including the little containers of supplies that would otherwise clutter your counter. Anything you regularly use and are likely to replace within 3–6 months will not be around long enough to be harmed by the humidity in the bath. Deodorant, toothpaste, shaving cream, and skin creams are all good candidates.

109
STORE YOUR MEDICINES SAFELY

The bathroom cabinet is not the best place to store medications because steam from the shower and bath can alter their effectiveness. Pull everything out and check expiration dates, then toss those with expired dates. (Don't flush medicines down the toilet—call your pharmacy to find out where you can locally dispose of the medications.) Move over-the-counter medications, vitamins, and prescription drugs to a cool, dry place out of the reach of children and teens.

110
CONQUER CLUTTER

Find a way to store shampoo, toothpaste, body wash, and lotions out of sight. A jumble of containers makes it harder to clean because gunk collects beneath. Perhaps more important to your sense of well-being, an uncluttered vanity top or bathtub surround makes the entire space appear to be clean. If all cabinets are packed full, look for attractive baskets that nest near the tub or vanity, keeping consolidated containers handy.

111
MAKE YOUR SHOWER SPARKLE

It may seem odd that a space that gets a daily dose of soap and water needs cleaning daily, but soap leaves scum and water leaves spots. It takes just a couple of minutes to avoid the time-consuming task of removing a thick layer of soap buildup. Scrub the shower walls, door, and tracks each week to remove mineral deposits.

SQUEEGEE EVERY DAY Before you leave the shower, spray the walls and doors with the Nonabrasive Vinegar Cleaner (see item 149) or a cleaner appropriate to the wall material (see note below) and use the squeegee to remove soap along with the cleaning solution. Follow the squeegee with a microfiber-cloth wipe, much like you wipe your windshield with paper towels after using the squeegee on it.

A CAUTIONARY TALE Vinegar is harmful to stone tile, such as slate, marble, granite, and travertine. Composite granite and quartz, as well as cultured marble, should also not be cleaned with vinegar. Use a solution of soap and water, squeegee, and dry.

SHOWER CURTAINS Liners and curtains can be washed with a mild detergent in cold water on the gentle cycle of a front-load washer, with ½ c. white vinegar in the machine's fabric-softener dispenser. Be cautious with a top-load washer—the agitator can damage the curtain with direct contact. Try adding a barrier of rags around the agitator, or spot-clean with the Nonabrasive Vinegar Cleaner (see item 149) and throughly rinse.

112
CLEAN YOUR SHOWERHEAD

Minerals can build up within the showerhead and impede the fast and straight flow of water, but cleaning the head is pretty easy if you just follow these steps.

STEP ONE Use a toothbrush or grout brush to scrub the showerhead once a month.

STEP TWO Every three months, fill a plastic bag with white distilled vinegar and tie the bag around the showerhead so the head is submerged in the vinegar.

STEP THREE Let it sit overnight, and the vinegar will start to dissolve the mineral buildup.

STEP FOUR Remove the bag and scrub the head with a toothbrush or microfiber cloth.

STEP FIVE Turn on the shower full blast to clear the showerhead.

114
GO AFTER GROUT

Stone and high-gloss ceramic tiles can be dulled by vinegar and lemon juice, so mix ¾ c. baking soda, ½ c. hydrogen peroxide, and 2 c. water to make a paste and apply it on the grout. Leave it for 15 minutes and then scrub with a grout brush, keeping within the lines. Rinse all traces away with warm water.

113 AIR IT OUT

Having an operational vent is key to removing excess moisture from the bathroom and is a preventative step to discourage mildew. But it works most efficiently if it's clean. At least twice a year, perform the following maintenance.

DISENGAGE Turn off the electricity to the bathroom.

REMOVE Secure a ladder beneath the vent and remove the vent cover. (Be prepared for dust and gunk to fall out.)

SOAK Submerge the vent cover in warm, soapy water.

VACUUM With a handheld mini-vac or a dust-brush attachment, vacuum the fan blades.

WIPE Dampen a microfiber cloth in warm, soapy water and wipe down each fan blade. You may need a toothbrush to clean otherwise inaccessible spots.

DRY Make sure the vent cover is dry before replacing it.

Quick Tip

PASS THE BAR

Soap scum results from the talc in bar soap. You'll have less soap scum if you opt for liquid body wash or glycerin soap.

115

KNOW YOUR BATHTUB

Whether it's the site of a nightly calming experience (think essential oils, soy candles, and bubbles) or a parental necessity (baby shampoo, rubber ducks, and bubbles), the bathtub needs to be clean and inviting. Here are dependable cleaning approaches tailored to the bathtub material of your home, with cleaning recipes you can find in item 149. And remember to periodically use the Disinfectant to sanitize your tub.

BATHTUB	CLEANING METHOD	TIPS & TRICKS	AVOID
ACRYLIC	Clean with mild soap and water. Rinse well. Dry to prevent water spotting.	Use a soft cloth and elbow grease on tough spots. Step up to the Nonabrasive Vinegar Cleaner if necessary.	Abrasive sponges and cleaners will scratch the surface.
COPPER AND NICKEL	Rinse well and dry after each use. Weekly, wash with mild soap and water. Rinse well and dry.	Copper and nickel with a protective coating need only rinsing and a quick wipe.	Abrasives will scratch. Acidic-cleaning products will pit copper.
CULTURED MARBLE, COMPOSITE GRANITE, ONYX, AND QUARTZ	Use only mild soap and a soft cloth. Rinse well and dry after every use.	Reseal the tub annually to diminish staining.	Avoid scouring pads and abrasive cleaning products, ammonia-based products, and bleach.
FIBERGLASS	Rinse and dry after every use. In hard-water areas, spray after every use with the Nonabrasive Vinegar Cleaner (see item 149), rinse, and dry.	Attack resistant stains with a baking soda paste.	Abrasive sponges and cleaners will scratch. Toys and bottles left in/on tub can stain.
MARBLE	Clean with mild soap and water after every use. Dry thoroughly.	Bath oils, shampoos, body washes, and shaving creams can discolor marble. Reseal annually to maintain stain resistance.	Never use abrasive or acidic materials.
PORCELAIN ENAMEL OVER CAST IRON OR STEEL	Clean with mild soap and water. Rinse and dry. For deeper cleaning, use the Tub 'n' Tile Cleaner (see Recipes at back of book).	For stains, dip half a lemon cut side down in baking soda and use it to scrub. Rinse and dry.	Avoid caustic chemical cleaning products.
SOLID SURFACE	Clean with warm, soapy water and a sponge. Rinse and dry.	For stains, use a nonabrasive scrubber with baking soda or vinegar.	Water that dries on the surface creates an unsightly film. Dry often.

116
TREAT YOUR TUB RIGHT

Freestanding tubs in which the tub's interior may be sheathed in a different material than its interior are in vogue: a porcelain interior with a stainless exterior, or a nickel interior with a copper exterior. Follow the recommendations in the bathtub chart (see item 115) for cleaning specific materials however they may be used. More common are built-in tub surrounds of wood, tile, or stone that support a drop-in tub. When cleaning, treat these materials as you would a wall (see items 023 and 026) or countertop (see items 089–090).

117
SANITIZE THE WHIRLPOOL

A relaxing luxury, a whirlpool tub requires thorough, regular cleaning to halt the growth of bacteria and mold. After each use, rinse it well and dry with a towel to eliminate lingering moisture.

Because they are easily molded, acrylic and fiberglass whirlpools are common, but check the chart (see item 115) for cleaning practices for your specific tub body. When possible, read and follow the manufacturer's instructions because many whirlpools have piping and jet designs that require specialized cleaning techniques.

At least once a month, clean and disinfect your whirlpool by following these simple steps. Knowing that your whirlpool is a beautiful and clean oasis will be motivation to enjoy it more.

STEP ONE Fill the tub with enough water to reach 3 in. above the jets, then add 1 c. white vinegar and 2 Tbsp. mild liquid soap.

STEP TWO Turn the whirlpool on for 15 minutes.

STEP THREE Drain the tub and refill again to 3 in. above the jets. This time, run the jets for 10 minutes before draining.

STEP FOUR Clean the individual jets by dipping a toothbrush in vinegar and scrubbing the holes. Rinse the toothbrush in water and rub within the holes to rinse away all gunk.

118
CLEAR DRAINS NATURALLY

Hair and soap scum readily clog bathroom drains, but fortunately, it's easy to get the water moving again without resorting to acidic chemical dissolvers. Commercial drain cleaners are highly toxic and will damage many sink, tub, and shower materials if you accidentally spill as you pour the solutions into the drain. Instead, try this method to dislodge clogs without the acrid smell and potential for damage.

BOIL Start an electric kettle with 2–3 qts. water, or bring to a boil in a large kettle on the stovetop.

COMBINE Mix 1 c. table salt and 1 c. baking soda and pour it down the drain.

BUBBLE Slowly pour 1 c. vinegar into the drain and let it bubble for a minute or two.

PURGE Clear the drain by pouring in the boiling water. Wipe the drain cover with a soft cloth to make sure no salt or vinegar remains.

Repeat these steps monthly and your pipes will stay clear, and you'll increase the probability that you can avoid serious trouble and costly calls to a professional plumber.

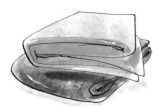

119
TAKE CARE OF YOUR TOWELS

We all love the scent of freshly laundered towels after an invigorating shower, so I make sure every towel in our house gets washed regularly. We don't wash them every day, because there's limited time, washing wears out the towel, and it's not environmentally responsible. If you take care of your towels, you only need to wash them after every three or four uses.

OWN Do not share towels among family members. Everyone should have their own hook or rack for hanging their towel until it's time for the weekly wash. A towel bar allows quicker air-drying than a hook.

DEHUMIDIFY Turn on the vent or open a window so that air circulates during and after the shower. It minimizes the moisture in the air, making the towels less hospitable to the growth of bacteria.

SMELL Be wary of stinky towels. When you smell moldy towels, wash them on the hottest setting, take them from the washer immediately after the cycle finishes, and put them in the dryer.

120
REMEMBER THE ROBE

Terry bathrobes can provide a degree of luxury to your postbath experience if they're soft, fluffy, and clean. As with towels, the challenge is to keep them fresh in a humid environment, especially when absorbing excess moisture from your body after a hot shower. But robes have an additional challenge: you may feel clean after that shower, but skin cells rub off onto the robe as you wear it. These cells build up and are vulnerable to bacteria growth and its accompanying smells.

To keep your terry bathrobe fresh, let it air out and thoroughly dry after each use. Bathrobes are similar to bath towels in that they won't dry well if left in a clump on the floor. It takes just a few seconds to hang your robe from a hook; if you don't have a designated place to keep your robe, make one. Adding another piece of bathroom hardware to the wall is simple enough for anyone to do, and will go a long way toward keeping your house tidy.

Wash your robe every time you wash your towels to maintain a hygienic routine, and tumble dry on low heat to fluff up the terry loops, which get matted down during the washing machine's spin cycle.

As with all textiles, consult the labels for specific care instructions, especially with silk and linen.

121
LAUNDER ALL BATH MATS

Fabric bath mats hold onto moisture and mold through repeated contact with wet feet and the bathroom floor, so wash them at least once a week. Even with a rubber backing, a mat can be machine-washed on a warm or cold setting. A rubber backing will fare better if the mat is hung outside to dry away from direct sunlight. If your bath mat does not have a rubber backing, machine-wash in hot water and then move it into the dryer.

Similarly, contour bath mats that fit around your toilet should be washed as directed above and dried according to whether it has a rubber backing.

122
CLEAN SINKS AND VANITY TOPS

Sinks and vanity tops are available in a dazzling assortment of materials and colors, and while a few materials have specific requirements for care, most are best cleaned with just a little soap and water. Cleaning and drying after every use are critical, however, to diminish water spotting. Clean as you go or work harder later.

Spread a mild liquid soap mixed with warm water on both the sink and the vanity counter, wiping with a sponge or microfiber cloth, then dry with another cloth. If you prefer something stronger, clean with the Disinfectant (see item 149).

123
FIRST, DO NO HARM

Whenever feasible, refer to the manufacturer's instructions for cleaning your particular sink material. Follow the guidelines below to keep these areas spotlessly clean while minimizing the risk of stains or discoloration.

WIPE Quickly wipe up toothpaste, lotions, and makeup, as they can stain.

DRY Rinse and dry with a towel after every use. While it may seem silly to dry a sink, it effectively diminishes water spotting,

AVOID Abrasive cleaning pads and commercial cleaners can scratch delicate surfaces, and bleach and ammonia-based cleaners can chemically damage surfaces.

PROTECT If commercial drain cleaners get on the surrounding sink, they can damage it. See item 118 for how to unclog your drain using all-natural materials.

Quick Tip

STAY FILM FREE

After giving your countertops a thorough cleaning, instead of air drying them, be sure to wipe them completely dry to avoid a buildup of film on the surface.

124
TREAT STAINS ON PORCELAIN

A material often used for sinks but rarely for countertops is porcelain enamel. For stains on porcelain enamel sinks as well as tubs, dip half of a lemon cut side down in baking soda and use it to scrub the stain. Rinse well and dry.

125
DECLUTTER DRAWERS AND CABINETS

All the nooks and crannies need to be seasonally cleaned and decluttered. Empty the drawers and cabinets so you can thoroughly vacuum all interior spaces with a dust-brush attachment. Then wipe with a soft cloth or sponge dampened with the All-Purpose Cleaner (see item 149). Use a toothbrush to clean the edges and corners. Wipe again with a cloth dampened with water to remove any trace of the cleaner. Let them dry completely before replacing the contents.

126
KEEP A MAKEUP DRAWER PRETTY

A pinch of face powder, a sprinkle of eye shadow, and a drop of foundation all accumulate in the makeup drawer in spite of our best efforts.

Remove everything, discarding old makeup and all those free samples you thought you'd try and never did. Makeup doesn't usually have a printed expiration date, although the rule of thumb for mascara is 6 months. Adopt that time period and toss things that have gone unused since then.

Rejuvenate the drawer itself by following the process in item 125. Wash all organizers and clean cosmetic bottles and tubes before returning them to the drawer. (Toss if they are a lost cause.)

127
TREASURE YOUR JEWELRY

Velvet-, felt-, or fabric-lined jewelry boxes and trays collect dust, and you'll be caught in a never-ending cycle of cleaning your jewelry unless you clean up their home. Follow these steps to keep your jewelry shining bright!

STEP ONE Close or cover your sink drain so you don't lose a favorite earring, then lay out a towel to protect both the counter and your jewelry as you empty the box or drawer.

STEP TWO Remove any drawer organizers or trays and clean the drawer (see item 126).

STEP THREE Use cotton swabs—dampened if needed—to get the dirt out of the cushioned compartment for rings and out of corners. Wipe all the fabric-lined surfaces with a barely damp microfiber cloth.

STEP FOUR For more cleaning power, vacuum with a dust brush or use compressed air to dislodge dust.

128
WIPE DOWN BATH FIXTURES

A quick wipe down daily will keep your bath fixtures looking like new. Most faucets and handles, shower hardware, and towel bars installed within the last 20 years have a factory-applied coating that is stain and tarnish resistant. You need only wipe the hardware with a soft cloth after every use to remove fingerprints and water spotting. Be diligent, because minerals in the water and soap scum left to sit will wear away the protective coating over time.

129
PRESERVE YOUR PROTECTION

Your overall goal with faucets and fixtures is to preserve their protective coating. If the applied coating is scratched or chipped, the base material is exposed to oxidization and can discolor. Stay away from abrasive cleaners and cleaning pads, bleach, ammonia, rubbing alcohol, acidic solutions, cleaning products designed to remove tarnish or rust, and polishes with harsh chemicals.

Many manufacturers use a physical-vapor-deposition (PVD) process or a clean protective coated finish on fixtures of brass, copper, bronze, stainless, chrome, or nickel, so it may be impossible to identify whether an existing fixture is coated.

130
CLEAN CLASSIC HARDWARE

Fixtures over 20 years old are probably uncoated, though they can still be scratched by abrasive scrubbers, so rely only on soft cloths and sponges. Start with soapy water, rinse well, dry, and buff. If needed, step up to the Nonabrasive Vinegar Cleaner (see item 149). Baking soda is a mild abrasive, and a baking soda paste is the next possibility for tough spots. Let it sit for 5 minutes, rinse with copious amounts of water to get rid of every trace of baking soda, dry, and buff.

133
GO FOR THE GOLD

Some luxury faucets are plated in gold, which is a soft finish without protective coating. To safely clean gold plate, spray a vinegar water solution (1 part vinegar to 3 parts water) on a soft cloth. Drape the cloth on the faucet or fixture and leave for 15 minutes. Gently rub with the wet cloth. Repeat if there is resistant dirt. Wipe with a water-soaked cloth, being sure to remove all of the vinegar solution. Dry with a fresh cloth.

131
LET A NATURAL PATINA DEVELOP

Uncoated brass, copper, and bronze, known as living finishes, are intended to change appearance over time. All of these are prized for the patina they develop with age and wear; just keep water spots and soap scum off of them and avoid commercial cleaners and abrasive pads.

132
PLAY IT SAFE

If you can identify the faucet's manufacturer, check its website for specific cleaning instructions. If you're cleaning blind and want to remove accumulated water spots or soap, start with warm, soapy water, rinse well to remove all traces of soap, dry, and buff with a microfiber cloth. A soft toothbrush can dislodge dirt that may build up around the joints.

134
REJUVENATE MAKEUP BRUSHES

Dainty makeup brushes can collect enough goop to render them useless. Rather than throwing them away and replacing them, simply follow these directions to give your brushes a makeover.

RINSE Once a week, run barely warm tap water over the bristles of each brush without getting the handles wet.

LATHER Pour a few drops of mild liquid soap into your palm and massage the soap through the bristles. Rinse until the water runs clean, repeating as needed.

WRING With your fingers or a towel, gently squeeze excess water out of the brushes.

DRY Lay the brushes flat on a towel to dry. If you stand them with brush end up, the water will drain into the handle and loosen the bristles.

135
FRESHEN YOUR TOOTHBRUSH

The American Dental Association recommends a thorough rinsing of your toothbrush in warm water after brushing and letting the brush air-dry in an upright position. If you want more assurance, soak the brush in an antiseptic mouthwash for 15 minutes.

136
SCRUB CANISTERS, CUPS, AND DISHES

Tumblers for rinsing, canisters for cotton balls or toothbrushes, and soap dishes should take a run through the dishwasher once a week. If they aren't dishwasher safe, follow the guidelines for materials often found in sink and vanity tops (see item 090).

One problematic item is the soap dish, which often is gummed up with soap scum. Follow these steps to clean and maintain for the future.

STEP ONE After emptying the soap dish, line it with a paste made from baking soda and water.

STEP TWO Let it sit for a few minutes and scrub it with a toothbrush (or abrasive sponge if it won't scratch the finish), and rinse clean.

STEP THREE Once it's clean, put a little baby oil in the soap dish to make it easier to clean the next time.

137
TEND TO A HAIRBRUSH

Just as you have to wash your hair to remove dirt, oil, and built-up hair product, so too does your hairbrush need periodic cleaning to remove the same. As you follow these steps, remember to remove loose hairs that have accumulated in the sink to prevent future drain clogs.

STEP ONE Run a comb through your hairbrush until you can't get any more hair out of the bristles.

STEP TWO Fill the sink with warm water and a few drops of your favorite shampoo, and swish the brush in the water for a few minutes.

STEP THREE Run a comb through the brush again to remove loosened hair.

STEP FOUR Drain the sink and rinse the brush with warm water.

STEP FIVE Let the brush dry naturally on a towel, bristles down, so that all the water can drain out.

Quick Tip

SAVE ON WASTE-CAN CLEANING

A small garbage bag saves you the time of cleaning out the interior. Take a hint from hotel maids and leave a few bags folded at the bottom of the can so they are always handy. Once a month, clean the inside of the can with the Disinfectant (see item 149).

SOAPS

138

TAKE ON THE TOILET

We all probably agree that this our least favorite cleaning project, one that tempts us to procrastinate. For our family's health and our own peace of mind, however, it must be done—regularly. Through daily practice, I've knocked this chore down into a reasonable process that I can speedily get through.

DAILY Follow the recipe for the Toilet Bowl Cleaner (see item 149), or toss in a couple of the Toilet Bowl Bombs (see item 149) if have unexpected company and you're pressed for time.

WEEKLY Flushing toilets scatters bacteria out of the bowl like a fountain, so the exterior needs a good weekly cleaning. Liberally spray with the Disinfectant (see item 149) and wipe clean, starting with the tank top and working down to the base.

MONTHLY Turn the water off at the safety valve beneath the tank and flush to empty both the bowl and tank.

Sprinkle baking soda around the inside of the bowl. Scrub the bowl and under the rim of the toilet to get rid of any dirt or stains. Pour 1 c. distilled vinegar around the inside of the bowl and let it sit for an hour.

Now it's time to clean the tank. Make a disinfectant spray of ¼ c. white vinegar to 1 c. water and spray on the walls of the empty tank. Start with a sponge or microfiber cloth to clean inside the tank and advance to a scrub brush and toothbrush if necessary to remove deposits. Turn on the water again and flush.

139
COPE WITH MINERAL DEPOSITS

Calcium, magnesium, and other minerals in your water will accumulate on the bowl, and how often you need to remove them depends on your water's composition. In hard-water areas, plan to add this step when you have the water off and the bowl empty for monthly cleaning.

SOAK Fill the toilet bowl with distilled white vinegar and leave it overnight. Use a sponge soaked in vinegar to access under the rim.

SCOUR The next day, scrub the stains with your toilet brush or a stiff natural-bristle brush.

ADVANCE For resistant water rings and mineral stains, consider using a wet pumice stone, but only as a last resort. Applying too much pressure on the stone will damage the bowl.

RINSE Turn on the water and flush. You may need to repeat these steps to get rid of all deposits.

REMEMBER The best protection is to remove the deposits often so they don't build up over time.

140
KEEP A BIDET PRISTINE

Bidets come in two varieties, conventional stand-alone units and add-on attachments that are often combined with a toilet seat. Follow the appropriate cleaning steps for your setup on a weekly basis.

Conventional Bidet

Traditional bidets can essentially be cleaned like your toilet bowl. Follow these steps to achieve good hygiene.

STEP ONE Squirt liquid castile soap under the rim, then sprinkle ½ c. baking soda into the bowl. Scrub with a toilet brush, and flush.

STEP TWO Run the bidet to make sure all the cleaning product is washed away, and let it air-dry.

STEP THREE Clean the exterior just as you would the toilet (see item 138).

STEP FOUR Wipe the controls or wireless remote with a clean microfiber cloth and the Disinfectant Spray.

STEP FIVE There are many variations on spray jets and nozzles, so consult with the manufacturer for the safest way to clean them.

Add-On Bidet

Before cleaning add-on bidet seats retrofitted on a toilet, unplug the unit to avoid shocks and potential electrical damage.

STEP ONE The seats are rigid plastic and should be cleaned only with mild soap and water. Harsh abrasives, alcohol, and bleach will cause discoloration and cracking and may void the warranty.

STEP TWO Mix a solution of 1 part soap to 4 parts water, and add 1 part vinegar if you want a natural disinfectant.

STEP THREE Dip a microfiber cloth into the solution and wring it out before wiping down all parts of the seat and control. Dip a Q-tip into the solution to clean tight spots.

STEP FOUR Wipe again with a damp cloth to remove all cleaning solution and let it air-dry before plugging it back in.

141
CLEAN THE TOILET BRUSH

The toilet brush wins the prize for the dirtiest tool in the house. Clean it weekly by soaking the toilet brush in pure vinegar inside the brush holder. Pour enough vinegar to cover the brush and leave it for several hours or overnight. After soaking, hold the brush over the toilet and pour the vinegar over it and into the bowl. Flush and rinse the brush in fresh water, and rinse the holder. Before returning the brush to its holder, put ¼ c. vinegar in the holder along with 10 drops tea tree oil. If you have pets, be sure to cover the solution.

142
CARE FOR SICK FAMILY MEMBERS

When someone becomes ill, assign them to a designated bedroom and, if possible, dedicate one bathroom for the patient's use only. If they are feeling up to being in the family room, label one chair or couch as only theirs for the duration.

143
QUARANTINE THE GERMS

If there is any time to be vigilant about general cleaning and especially cleaning the bathroom, it's when someone in your house gets sick. Speed healing, prevent contagion, and maintain some control by implementing a get-well-quick triage routine.

144
LAUNDER IN HOT WATER

Wash pillowcases, pajamas, hand towels, and—if practical—sheets every day. After the patient is feeling better, also wash blankets, duvet covers, and couch throws.

145
WASH YOUR HANDS

Washing with hand soap for 20–25 seconds is as critical as all other efforts to keep from spreading illness. During your routine, scrub your fingertips into your opposite palms or use a nail brush to get germs hiding under your fingernails. Wash often and remind the rest of the household to do the same!

146
CONSIDER DISPOSABLES

Although I'm a proponent of minimizing waste and maximizing conservation efforts, this is a time when it makes sense to use paper towels and disposable wipes. Cloth wipes may, in fact, help spread germs and must be changed often.

147
STERILIZE SURFACES

At the end of the day, walk through the house with an eye toward anything the patient may have touched. Adhere to the directions and cautions specific to materials throughout this book, but follow these general guidelines. While vinegar and hydrogen peroxide are mild disinfectants, they do not kill all types of germs and bacteria. Follow up with hot, soapy water for maximum effectiveness. Clean doorknobs, light switches, cabinet handles, and the fridge door. Spray sinks and counters, toilets, and floors with the Nonabrasive Vinegar Cleaner (see 149) and then wash with hot, sudsy water.

148
DISINFECT EVERYTHING

After every use, wipe the thermometer with rubbing alcohol and let it air-dry before putting it away. Dip the patient's toothbrush in hydrogen peroxide and isolate it from other brushes.

Dampen cotton pads with hydrogen peroxide and wipe frequently handled devices that may get overlooked, such as:

- ☐ Cell phones and tablets
- ☐ Computer keyboards and mouses
- ☐ Ebook readers
- ☐ Radio and stereo knobs
- ☐ Remote controls
- ☐ Videogame controllers

149 MAKE BATHROOM CLEANSERS

With a little TLC, your bathroom can be an oasis in your home. Use these natural cleaning products to help disinfect, deodorize, and cut through any soapy buildup.

DISINFECTANT 2 Tbsp. liquid castile soap, 20 drops tea tree oil.

Mix the soap and essential oil with hot water in a 16-oz. spray bottle.

NONABRASIVE VINEGAR CLEANER
1 part distilled white vinegar, 2 parts water, 5 drops lavender essential oil.

Combine the vinegar and water in a 16-oz. spray bottle. Add 5 drops of essential oils if you don't like the smell of vinegar—my favorites are lavender, grapefruit, orange, lemon, and peppermint.

TOILET BOWL BOMBS
1½ c. baking soda, ½ c. citric acid powder, 20 drops peppermint essential oil

Thoroughly mix the baking soda and citric acid powder in a bowl. Slowly stir in the peppermint essential oil to evenly distribute. Use a spray bottle to sparingly mist water to the mixture—stirring to uniformly moisten the powder—until the powder will stick together in clumps. The mixture will slightly fizz from the moisture, so make sure not to oversaturate.

Firmly pack a silicone mold with the moist mixture and

leave out to dry overnight, wiping off any excess from the fizzing. Gently remove the formed bombs from the mold and store in a sealable container.

Add a finished bomb to the toilet bowl and allow to fizz. Once the bomb has dissolved, flush out the bowl water.

TOILET BOWL CLEANER
Liquid castile soap, baking soda

Squirt the liquid castile soap under the rim of the toilet bowl, then sprinkle ½ c. baking soda into the bowl. Scrub with a toilet brush, and flush to rinse.

BATHROOM
Checklists

Keeping the bathroom clean on a daily basis is much easier than cleaning it every once in a while. Train your family to wipe down faucets, sinks, the shower, and the tub after every use. You can whisk through the rest in 5 minutes a day.

Numbers refer to the general cleaning entries, so make sure to reference the appropriate supporting items to address specific materials and circumstances.

DAILY

- ☐ Sweep or vacuum floors *30*
- ☐ Put dirty clothes in hamper *105*
- ☐ Wipe faucets *105*
- ☐ Wipe sinks and counters *105*
- ☐ Squeegee shower *105*
- ☐ Rinse bathtub *105*
- ☐ Rinse and dry whirlpool *105*
- ☐ Swish toilets *138*
- ☐ _____

WEEKLY

- ☐ Clean mirrors *13*
- ☐ Dust window treatments *14*
- ☐ Dust doors and baseboards *18*
- ☐ Clean switch plates *19*
- ☐ Dust ceilings and walls *20*
- ☐ Mop floors *31*
- ☐ Freshen air *107*
- ☐ Scrub shower *111*
- ☐ Deep-clean tub *115*
- ☐ Clean sink *122*
- ☐ Wash towels, bathmats, and bathrobes *119*
- ☐ Wash makeup and hair brushes *134*
- ☐ Wash canisters, glasses, soap dishes *136*
- ☐ Wipe down toilet exterior and tank *138*
- ☐ Clean bidet *140*
- ☐ Clean toilet brush *141*

MONTHLY

- ☐ Clean window treatments *14*
- ☐ Wash trash bins *28*
- ☐ Sanitize whirlpool tub *117*
- ☐ Clear drains *118*
- ☐ Clean tub exterior *116*
- ☐ Deep-clean toilet bowl and tank *138*
- ☐ Remove minerals from toilet *139*
- ☐ _____

SEASONALLY (SPRING AND FALL)

- ☐ Wash windows *12*
- ☐ Deep-clean window treatments *14*
- ☐ Wipe doors and baseboards *18*
- ☐ Clean walls *20*
- ☐ Clean sconces and light fixtures *54, 57*
- ☐ Restock bathroom caddy *106*
- ☐ Remove clutter *110*
- ☐ Purge medicine cabinet *108*
- ☐ Wash shower curtain *111*
- ☐ Clean showerhead *112*
- ☐ Clean vent *113*
- ☐ Clean grout *114*
- ☐ Clean shelves, drawers, and cabinets *125*
- ☐ Clean makeup drawer *126*
- ☐ Clean jewelry box *127*

The laundry room is the workhorse of the house.
It's a fundamental part of housekeeping and an area that needs to remain clean and organized in order to function properly. If you have piles of laundry in the middle of the floor and a mildew smell coming out of the washing machine, I bet your life is more than chaotic. The laundry room represents ones state of mind. If all your laundry is washed, folded, and put away daily and the laundry room is clean, you probably feel more at ease. That is the best feeling in the world. Throughout this section, you will learn how keep up with the laundry, save money by making your own laundry detergent, maintain and clean your washer and dryer, and tackle hard-to-clean stains. Laundry doesn't have to be a chore. It can be quite enjoyable, especially if you have a solid routine in place and helping hands nearby.

150
DO LAUNDRY RIGHT

Few things are as satisfying as fresh, clean-smelling laundry neatly folded and then delivered to appropriate shelves, drawers, and closets. Over the years, as my family grew, I learned how to keep laundry from becoming an overwhelming task I wanted to put off. The trick is this: Don't let the clothes stack up. It really is as simple as that. As soon as I'm up and dressed each morning, I start one load of laundry and dry, fold, and put it away before day's end. I keep the laundry room clear with regular tidying and more in-depth attention to appliances every few months. In this section, I'm sharing other useful practices that help me enjoy getting the laundry done quickly and efficiently.

Quick Tip
STYLE YOUR SPACE

Extend your home decor into the laundry room. It will help make laundry days more enjoyable. Hang a favorite collection (or start a collection) of old sock drying stretchers, washboards, or vintage photographs of washday. Make this room a place you enjoy spending time in. The top shelf of my laundry room is primarily for my farmhouse-style decor, and I love it.

151
ORGANIZE THE LAUNDRY ROOM

Consolidating and purging laundry room clutter are the first step to maintaining a clean space. Organize cleaning supplies and related items in linen-lined baskets with labels. Use antique wire baskets or enamel trays to store laundry supplies. Once you organize your supplies, keeping it clean will be the easy part.

153
STEAM-CLEAN AN IRON

The flat metal base of the iron that becomes hot—known as the soleplate—can get gummed up with starch and mineral deposits. A similar buildup in the steam holes can decrease the iron's effectiveness and cause the iron to snag delicate blouses or shirts. Avoid this potentially costly problem by cleaning your iron at least once a year.

STEP ONE Set the heat to the highest setting (with the steam option disabled). Pour kosher or rock salt on top of a large paper bag and iron over the salt to dislodge anything stuck to the soleplate. Repeat with new salt until the soleplate is clean. Turn off the heat, let the iron cool, and wipe the soleplate.

STEP TWO Make a paste from 2 Tbsp. baking soda and 1 Tbsp. water, and spread it over the cold soleplate and

152
SET UP A CATCHALL BASKET

Treasures are revealed when pockets are emptied, and it's handy to have one place to put them. Let everyone in the family know where they can retrieve coins, lip balm, and mass-transit passes.

into the steam holes. After a few minutes, wipe the soleplate clean with a damp microfiber cloth.

STEP THREE Use a cotton swab dampened with distilled water to clean out the steam holes. If they're still clogged from mineral deposits, dip the cotton swab in white vinegar and rub into the holes to dissolve mineral buildup.

STEP FOUR Fill the water reservoir with distilled water. Turn on the heat to the highest setting (with the steam option activated). When the iron is hot, press the steam button to flush out impurities.

If you live in a hard-water area, consider adding a mixture of ¼ c. white vinegar to ¾ c. distilled water into the reservoir for this process, but check the owner's manual to ensure you don't damage the iron.

STEP FIVE Turn off the iron and let it cool, use a damp microfiber cloth to wipe away any debris that was pushed out by the steam, and empty the reservoir after cleaning.

154

DEAL WITH TOUGH STAINS

Before you launch into treating a stain, remember these suggestions to make sure you do more good than harm.

KNOW Read the garment's care label for specific instructions and cautions.

SAMPLE Test in an unnoticeable place in case your technique has adverse effects.

CHILL Always rinse and soak stains in cold water—warm or hot water can set the stain.

REFRAIN Never scrub stains, or risk spreading the stain and fraying fibers.

ACCOMPLISH Remove the stain before laundering.

CONFIRM Air-dry after laundry to be certain stain is gone.

PRESERVE Don't put the garment in the dryer until the stain is completely removed. Heat from a dryer or iron will set the stain permanently.

ENLIST Wool, silk, other delicate fabrics and garments labeled "Dry Clean Only" should be turned over to a dry cleaner. Once you've worked on a stain unsuccessfully, the dry cleaner has less of a chance to get it out, so when in doubt, consult with a professional.

155

STOCK UP ON STAIN BUSTERS

You never know when a flick of mud or speckle of spaghetti sauce will strike, but any stain is easier to conquer while it is fresh. Be prepared so you can get a jump on accidents by creating a toolbox of stain-fighting products and ingredients in one basket. My first aid kit for stains includes the following:

BAKING SODA

CLUB SODA

CORNSTARCH

COTTON BALLS

CREAM OF TARTAR

DISHWASHING SOAP (CLEAR)

DISTILLED WHITE VINEGAR

SALT, BOTH TABLE AND KOSHER

HYDROGEN PEROXIDE

LIQUID LAUNDRY SOAP

PETROLEUM JELLY

RUBBING ALCOHOL

PLASTIC SPOON

EYEDROPPER

156

GO NATURAL

All the stain-removing solutions here use only natural ingredients, because I have banned toxic chemicals from our house. Commercial laundry products are among the most caustic, endangering our environment and our families. These more responsible methods work on all washable fabrics. And don't give up too quickly—it sometimes takes patience and several tries before a stain comes out.

STAIN	METHOD FOR REMOVAL
BABY FORMULA SPIT-UP	Gently scrape away excess surface spittle with a plastic spoon. Sprinkle with baking soda, then pour club soda over the baking soda. Once the fizzing stops, launder, then air-dry. If the stain is still there, repeat.
BIRD DROPPINGS	Scrape away droppings with a plastic spoon. Hold the stained fabric under cold running water. On colorfast fabrics, apply hydrogen peroxide with an eyedropper and rinse.
BLOOD	Hold the spot under cold running water for a minute to rinse out excess blood. Soak in cold water for 30 minutes. Apply dishwashing liquid to the stain. Gently work the soap into the stain and rinse with cold water. Repeat until the stain is gone.
CANDLE WAX	Scrape off excess wax with a plastic spoon. (If the wax is still soft, put fabric in the freezer to harden the wax.) On an ironing board, sandwich the fabric between paper towels or brown paper bags. Set an iron on low heat with no steam. Apply the iron, whose heat will transfer the wax to the paper towel or the bag. Repeat as necessary with new towels or bags. If a stain remains because of colored wax, apply a small amount of rubbing alcohol to the stain, dab, and rinse with cold water. Repeat until the stain is gone.
CHOCOLATE	Scrape chocolate off with a plastic spoon. Dab to remove any liquid. Carefully rub liquid laundry detergent on the stain so as not to spread it. Let the detergent sit for 5–10 minutes. Soak it in cold water for 15 minutes. The stain should be gone, but if not, repeat the process until it is.
COLA	Use a cloth or paper towel to remove as much liquid as possible, then apply white vinegar to the spot and blot. Add a small amount of diluted dishwashing liquid and gently work it in. Rinse well and blot to remove excess moisture. If the stain is still apparent, treat with hydrogen peroxide from an eyedropper and let it stand for an hour, then rinse.
CRAYON	Put the garment in a plastic bag, then place in the freezer for 30 minutes to harden the wax before gently scraping excess off. On an ironing board, sandwich the fabric between paper towels or brown paper bags with the crayon side down. With the iron on a low setting and no steam, place the iron on the top towel or bag. As the crayon melts, it will transfer to the bottom towel or bag, so replace it often. Repeat as necessary with new towels or bags.
DEODORANT	Rub deodorant streaks off clothes with nylon hose, cotton socks, or soft foam (the kind that comes on metal hangers from the dry cleaner).
FECES	Scrape off as much as possible with a plastic spoon. Rinse under cold running water. Fill a basin with water as hot as the fabric can tolerate; add 1 c. hydrogen peroxide and 1 c. baking soda. Agitate as much as possible, so the solution can dislodge the stain. Let it soak overnight. If the stain is gone, launder with the Powdered Laundry Detergent (see item 159)—it includes washing soda which helps neutralize and eliminate the odor. Air dry.

STAIN	METHOD FOR REMOVAL
GRASS	Using an eyedropper or cotton ball, pretreat the stain with rubbing alcohol. Rinse in cold water. Make a paste with a small amount of water and 2 Tbsp. Powdered Laundry Detergent (see 159). Cover the stain and let it sit for 15–20 minutes before laundering. Let it air-dry and check to make sure all pigment is gone. If not, apply the paste described below for removing red clay and launder again.
GUM	Fold clothing to fit within a plastic bag while leaving the gum exposed on top so it doesn't stick to the bag. Alternatively, lay the fabric on top of a cookie sheet. Place it in the freezer for 3–4 hours. Remove and open the bag, and use a plastic spoon to remove the hardened gum.
INK AND PERMANENT MARKER	Contain the ink by applying a circle of petroleum jelly around it. Lay down the ink-contact side of the fabric on a paper towel to absorb the stain. Use an eyedropper to saturate the stain with rubbing alcohol, and dab with cotton balls. Move the towel to a new, dry spot often. Add more alcohol and continue tamping until all is absorbed into the towels. It can take a while. If any ink remains, spot-treat with dishwashing detergent and let it sit 15–20 minutes before laundering. Air-dry.
KETCHUP	Scrape off as much as possible without spreading the stain. Run cold water from the back of the stain toward the front so the ketchup does not absorb further into the fibers. Apply laundry detergent to any remaining stain and work it in with your fingers. Consider soaking in cold, soapy water for 30 minutes. Rinse with cold water. If the stain is still visible, apply white vinegar with an eyedropper and repeat working in dishwashing detergent. Rinse again. If that hasn't cleared the redness, apply a little hydrogen peroxide with an eyedropper and let it sit for a while before working in more dishwashing detergent.
LIPSTICK	Scrape excess lipstick from the surface with the edge of a plastic spoon. Treat the stain from the backside of the garment and place a towel underneath it to absorb the stain. Drop rubbing alcohol from an eyedropper onto the stain and dab with a dry cloth or paper towel. Repeat until all color is gone.
MUD	Let the mud dry and scrape off any excess with a plastic spoon. Apply a small amount of laundry detergent to the stain and work it in. Leave it for 15 minutes. Wet a toothbrush and scrub to loosen the stain, working from both the inside and the outside of the fabric. Rinse with cold water when you feel the stain is sufficiently dislodged. Launder and air-dry.
MUSTARD	Scrape excess mustard from clothing with a plastic spoon. Working with the garment backside out, use an eyedropper to saturate the area with white vinegar. When most of the color is gone, work dishwashing liquid into the stain and rinse until all color has disappeared. Repeat with white vinegar and liquid soap if needed.
OIL	Immediately sprinkle corn starch onto the stain to absorb the oil. Let sit for 15 minutes, then brush away and saturate the spot with rubbing alcohol. Blot away excess moisture and work liquid dishwashing soap into the stain. Rinse well, and repeat with rubbing alcohol if necessary.

STAIN	METHOD FOR REMOVAL
PERSPIRATION STAINS	On white or light garments, mix 1 c. hydrogen peroxide with 1 c. water in a spray bottle and saturate the stain. Let it sit for 30 minutes. Rinse and launder in cold water. For darker staining on light garments, consider adding 1 c. hydrogen peroxide to a normal laundry load. For colored fabrics that may get bleached by hydrogen peroxide, mix 2 Tbsp. white vinegar with 1 c. water and saturate the stained area. Let it sit for 30 minutes before laundering.
RED CLAY	Scrape dried clay off with a plastic spoon and a dry toothbrush. On colored fabric, make a paste of ¼ c. table salt to ¼ c. white vinegar. Apply it to the stain and let rest for 20 minutes. Rinse off the paste and launder normally. Repeat if the stain has not disappeared. On white fabric, mix 1 Tbsp. cream of tartar, 1 tsp. baking soda, and just enough lemon juice to form a paste. Apply it to the stain and leave the fabric in the sun until the paste dries. Scrape off the paste. Launder normally and air-dry. Repeat if the stain persists.
RED WINE	Club soda won't remove red wine, but it can make it easier to clean later, so it's still a good emergency measure if you're out at a restaurant. At home, pour table salt on the stain and let it rest for an hour. Pour boiling water through the stain. Repeat as needed.
RUST	Lay fabric on an old towel and pour white vinegar or lemon juice on the stain (or make a paste of salt and lemon juice). Blot the stain with a clean white towel, and repeat if necessary. Lay fabric in direct sun, and once the stain disappears, launder and air dry.
SOY SAUCE	Blot stain with a clean white cloth. Rinse from the backside of the fabric. Dab the front of the stain with white vinegar, then hydrogen peroxide. Let it sit, then rinse. Launder normally and air dry.
TOOTHPASTE	Carefully scrape away toothpaste from stain with a plastic spoon. Apply detergent and water to a clean cloth or sponge and dab toothpaste until it disappears, then rinse.
URINE	Fill a bucket or the sink with 1 part white vinegar to 2 parts hot water (cold water if the fabric is delicate). Soak the urine-stained fabric for 45 minutes. Remove and rinse. If the stain is gone, launder using the Powdered Laundry Detergent (see item 159), which includes washing soda which helps neutralize and eliminate the odor, and air dry.
WATER-BASED GLUE	Let the glue dry. Soak in room-temperature water for 24 hours to soften. Wipe glue with a clean, dry cloth to protect fabric that might weaken with scrubbing. Launder normally in warm water and air-dry.

157 DECODE COMMON LAUNDRY SYMBOLS

Universal laundry symbols are increasingly replacing written care instructions on garment tags. In a global economy, a knit shirt manufactured in one country may be shipped to six nations with different languages. Universal pictograms graphically illustrate the cleaning processes best suited to the fabric. Here's a primer on how to read the symbols.

WASH	BLEACH	TUMBLE DRY	DRY	IRON	DRY CLEAN
Cool/Cold	Any Bleach	No Heat	Line Dry	Low	Do Not Dry Clean
Warm	Nonchlorine	Low	Drip Dry	Medium	
Hot	No Bleach	Medium	Dry Flat	High	
Normal		High	Dry in Shade	No Steam	
Permanent Press		Any Heat	Do Not Dry	Do Not Iron	
Delicate		Do Not Tumble Dry	Do Not Wring		
Hand-Wash					
Do Not Wash					

158 KNOW WHAT THE NUMBERS MEAN

It's simple to understand the care symbols of a shirt you bought during your Paris vacation or the blouse ordered from a Spanish website. The European wash-temperature symbols indicate the maximum recommended water temperature in Celsius, and use horizontal bars instead of vertical bars for the recommended type of cycle. It's that easy!

Quick Tip

USE YOUR JUDGMENT

The symbols identify the most aggressive cleaning possible without damaging a garment, but you can use gentler methods and temperatures if you think it best. For instance, the symbol may indicate that hot water is acceptable, but you may prefer to wash in warm or cold water.

And if you like the whitening power of industrial bleach yet are wary of its harsh chemicals, try using my Bleaching Solution (see Recipes at back of book) instead—it's much less toxic and can help brighten your whites!

159 MAKE YOUR OWN SUPPLIES

The laundry room is a place to get clothes clean, but these products will help you keep your appliances clean, too. And with the simple homemade laundry detergent recipe below, you can forego expensive retail detergents while maintaining their cleaning power!

ALL-PURPOSE CLEANER

2 tsp. borax, ¼ tsp. liquid castile soap, 10 drops lemon essential oil.

Mix all ingredients with hot water in a 16-oz. spray bottle.

NONABRASIVE VINEGAR CLEANER

1 part white vinegar
2 parts water
16 oz spray bottle

Combine the vinegar and water in a 16-oz. spray bottle. Add 5 drops of essential oils if you don't like the smell of vinegar—my favorites are lavender, grapefruit, orange lemon, and peppermint.

POWDERED LAUNDRY DETERGENT

3 bars of Dr. Bronner's or Fels Naphtha
   soap (shredded)
1 (4 lb.) box of super washing soda
1 (4 lb.) box of borax
1 (4 lb.) box of baking soda

Shred the soap in a food processor or with a cheese grater. Mix all ingredients in a large, sealable container.

Directions: Use 2 heaping tablespoons in a top-load machine, less for an HE washer.

160
WASH THE WASHER

All that warm water mixed with dirty fabrics takes a toll on the machine and can foster mold and mildew—something that often goes unnoticed until your clothes develop a musty smell. For deep cleaning, I add 1 c. bleach directly into the drum (per the manufacturer's instructions), and then run the machine on its hottest cycle. This is one of the only times I use bleach, and it works great to kill mildew. Check your owner's manual before doing a similar deep cleaning.

161
SOFTEN UP

You can achieve soft towels and clothes without the challenges that accompany chemical fabric softeners. Liquid fabric softener—as well as dryer sheets—coat your clothes with chemical compounds that cause the threads to extend, creating that luxurious fluffy softness. But that coating can build up and make fibers less absorbent. Instead, simply put ½ c. white vinegar in the fabric softener dispenser so it's added during the rinse cycle. The white vinegar is just acidic enough to dissolve fabric softener buildup, as well as detergent residue and hard-water mineral deposits that make towels feel scratchy and rough. Adding this small amount of vinegar to your rinse cycle will make your clothes soft, smell fresh, and be fully absorbent.

162
FRONT-LOAD YOUR LAUNDRY

Front-load washing machines use less energy and water, but they can smell funky if they are not cleaned often. The rubber gasket around the door of front loaders is more substantial than on top-loaders because it must hold back sloshing water. It's in that gasket that mold and mildew thrive on moisture and soap residue. Some models have a self-cleaning option, but you should still check the gasket for mold.

STEP ONE Wipe the gasket (and whatever area around the rubber gasket you can reach) with the Nonabrasive Vinegar Cleaner (see item 159) and a microfiber cloth. Pull the gasket back to clean the inside where mold grows. Because acidic vinegar can potentially deteriorate some rubber, wash the gasket, inside and out, with a wet cloth. Dry with a clean microfiber cloth to halt the growth of mold.

STEP TWO Select settings for a large load, extra-heavy soiling, and hot water. Fill the detergent dispenser to its maximum level with vinegar (or use ¾ c., whichever is greater) and start the cycle. Also, run a second cycle on rinse to make sure all the vinegar is removed from the drum.

STEP THREE Remove all dispensers (detergent, bleach, and fabric softener) and filters and wash them in the sink in warm, soapy water. Rinse, dry, and replace.

STEP FOUR Spray the Nonabrasive Vinegar Cleaner onto a microfiber cloth and wipe the exterior. Scrub tight, dirty areas with a toothbrush.

163
TAKE IT FROM THE TOP

If you have a top-load washer, follow these suggestions for cleaning your machine (after you've checked your owner's manual). A top loader's design requires a different approach in order to clean the top of the tub.

STEP ONE Set the cycle for the hottest temperature, largest load, and maximum soil level, then start the machine. Once it's full of water, add 1 qt. vinegar. Let the machine do its thing for several minutes to mix the solution. Pause the cycle by opening the lid.

STEP TWO Let the machine rest for 1–2 hours to let the vinegar work on the mold and mildew before restarting the machine to finish its cycle. Run an additional rinse to make certain that all the vinegar drains out of the drum.

STEP THREE Remove all dispensers (detergent, bleach, and fabric softener) and filters and wash them in the sink in warm, soapy water. Rinse, dry completely, and replace.

STEP FOUR Spray the Nonabrasive Vinegar Cleaner onto a microfiber cloth and wipe the exterior. Scrub tight, dirty areas with a toothbrush.

A front-loading washer's door gasket traps moisture that can lead to mold and mildew, so only close the door after you've let it air-dry.

164
SHOW YOUR DRYER SOME LOVE

The hug of warm towels that emerge fresh from the dryer is something I look forward to every time I do laundry. And the more quickly I collect the laundry once the dryer cycle ends, the less ironing and smoothing I'll have to do later. But dryers need maintenance or the lint filter can become a fire hazard. And even if you always clean the lint filter, fibers will inevitably get through and clog your exhaust line over time.

165

ADD A LITTLE BOUNCE

Dryer balls, by bouncing around among your clothes and pushing individual garments apart, create better air circulation. But they can also be used to add a fresh scent in lieu of dryer sheets.

ADD Toss three wool dryer balls and a load of wet clothes into the dryer. Run the dryer cycle as usual.

SCENT Once the load is dry, take the dryer balls out and add 1–2 drops of essential oil to each wool ball. My favorite essential oils to freshen clothes are lemongrass and lavender.

TUMBLE Throw the dryer balls back into the dryer with the load run on the no-heat cycle for 5 minutes, which will enable the delightful scents to transfer to your clothes.

166
KEEP DRYER VENTS CLEAN

The dryer's venting system is designed to exhaust heat and moisture to the outside. Even if you consistently clear the lint trap, lint particles can accumulate at other places along the exhaust system—as fine as your lint screen is, some lint particles will still be finer. One early tip-off to a clogged vent is that your clothes don't seem to dry in one cycle. Rather than risk a fire, attend to the dryer every six months.

DISASSEMBLE Unplug the dryer and pull it away from the wall. Remove the exhaust hose. If it's flexible, scrunch it up and vacuum inside, or clean the inside with a rag.

CLEAR Depending on the make of your dryer, you may have to take off the entire back panel, or you may be able to remove only the vent clamp and duct off the back. Reach into the vent on the back and pull out as much lint as you can. With a dust-brush attachment, vacuum any lint or dust you see. Vacuum the floor, then mop it and dry it before reattaching all parts and pushing the dryer back into place.

CLEAN Spray the drum with the Nonabrasive Vinegar Cleaner and wipe clean with a microfiber cloth. Wash the lint filter in warm, soapy water, scrubbing nasty corners with a toothbrush. While it's out, vacuum the lint that accumulates in its cavity. If possible, remove the lint-trap cover and vacuum.

RETURN Rinse and dry completely before replacing the filter. Spray the exterior and control panels with the Nonabrasive Vinegar Cleaner and wipe it clean with a microfiber cloth.

167
FILTER OUT LINT

What, exactly, is lint? It's not just stray threads from garments but also tiny fragments of threads and fibers formed from everyday wear, as well as fiber fragments from those stray receipts that somehow get past your laundry vigilance. Unlike fabric, in which long fibers are woven together and overlap, lint's fibers are short and independent, so there is much more surface area exposed. And that transforms all the individual fibers into a collection of kindling, which can ignite from the dryer's heat.

Quick Tip

MAKE YOUR OWN DRYER SHEETS

If you don't use dryer balls but still want to add a natural fragrance to your laundry, place 10 drops of pure essential oil on a cotton cloth and place in the dryer with your clothes after they are dry. Circulate on a no-heat cycle for 5 minutes. Whether you use clove, lime, spearmint, geranium, peppermint, spruce, or lavender, your clothes will have a fresh scent!

LAUNDRY
Checklists

Chances are good that your daily and weekly laundry routines are pretty well established. If you're not giving your laundry room the attention it needs to stay in tip-top working order, use this list to set up a maintenance schedule.

Numbers refer to the general cleaning entries, so make sure to reference the appropriate supporting items to address specific materials and circumstances.

DAILY

☐ Sweep or vacuum floors *30*
☐ Declutter laundry room *150*
☐ Spot-treat stains *156*
☐ Wash clothes *150*
☐ Dry clothes *165*

☐ Clean lint filter *166*
☐ _____
☐ _____
☐ _____

WEEKLY

☐ Dust window treatments *14*
☐ Dust doors and baseboards *18*
☐ Clean switch plates *19*
☐ Dust ceilings and walls *20*
☐ Mop floors *31*
☐ Wipe down washer and dryer

☐ _____
☐ _____
☐ _____
☐ _____
☐ _____
☐ _____
☐ _____

MONTHLY

☐ Clean window treatments *14*
☐ Wash trash bins *28*
☐ Clean doorknobs *29*
☐ Clean washer *160*

☐ Clean sink *122*
☐ Sweep and mop behind washer and dryer
☐ _____

SEASONALLY (SPRING AND FALL)

☐ Wash windows *12*
☐ Deep-clean window treatments *14*
☐ Wipe doors and baseboards *18*
☐ Clean walls *20*
☐ Clean sconces and light fixtures *54, 57*
☐ Clean iron *153*
☐ Clean washer *162, 163*
☐ Clean dryer vent *166*
☐ Restock the cleaning caddy *1*
☐ Restock laundry supplies *155, 159*

☐ _____
☐ _____
☐ _____
☐ _____
☐ _____
☐ _____
☐ _____
☐ _____
☐ _____
☐ _____

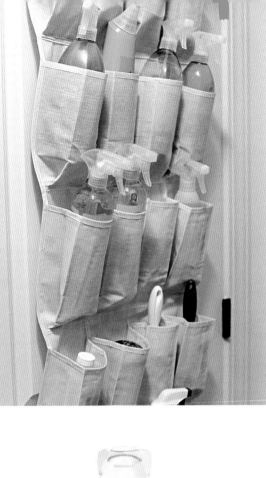

Living Spaces

Prepare your home for what life throws at it.

Your living spaces may be on the formal side, full of antiques and fine art, or they may be casual and comfortable with quilts or knitted blankets folded over the sofa. Both styles require consistent cleaning to be ready for your family's daily activities. In this chapter, I'll give you advice on cleaning spots and spills on upholstered furniture, dusting and polishing antiques and new wood, cleaning the fireplace (it's a messy job, but somebody's got to do it), and even how to take care of fine art. The trick to maintaining a clean home is to minimize and prevent excessive clutter, and to maintain a cleaning routine that fits your schedule. Keep the spaces clean and the tasks mastered, so that you can take a well-earned deep breath and relax with family and friends or simply watch Netflix while sipping a glass of wine.

168
LOVE YOUR LIVING ROOM

Whether your living room is formal or a more casual hangout, its purpose is clear: This is the spot where you gather for conversation, cocktail parties, breakfast meetings, and socializing. It should be as pretty as it is comfortable, and it's one of those rooms that should always be ready for company. You never know who will show up!

169
CLEAR OUT THE CLUTTER

If you've read my first book, *The Complete Book of Home Organization*, you already know how to minimize clutter. The information in these books goes hand-in-hand: It's challenging to clean if surfaces are covered, and it's disheartening to put away dirty things. My organizational recommendations are beyond the scope of this cleaning book, but do remember that eliminating clutter is your first line of defense in cleaning the living room!

170
KEEP DUST AT BAY

Take a pass over furniture and decor every few days to keep dust and cobwebs at bay. Keep it simple and use a slightly dampened microfiber cloth, working from top to bottom. Dust is the first thing you see, particularly if your living room is a formal space that doesn't get regular traffic and the light is streaming just the right (or wrong) way, so regular care is essential.

171

DEEP-CLEAN YOUR SOFA

Between everyday use that wears and fades upholstered furniture and spills that leave a mark, the sofa gets a lot of wear. You can always send it out to be dry-cleaned, but a more efficient and environmentally responsible alternative is cleaning the sofa yourself.

STEP ONE Find the manufacturer's care tag on the sofa to see its recommended method of overall cleaning. (See item 172 for help in decoding the care instructions.)

STEP TWO Vacuum the sofa surface, the cushions, the sofa body below the cushions (where pocket change and remote controls hide), and behind and under the sofa. Then brush with a bristled brush, dislodging any dirt, following the path of the vacuum so as not to miss any area. Vacuum the dislodged dirt.

STEP THREE Go over the sofa and cushions with a lint roller, following the path of the vacuum and brush. This will pull up stubborn pet hair and fur and resistant dust.

STEP FOUR Spray the All-Purpose Cleaner (see item 197) on a microfiber cloth to clean exposed wood and metal areas.

STEP FIVE Once you have vacuumed every trace of dust and surface dirt and hair from the furniture, attack the stains by spot-cleaning. If the manufacturer's code is a W or SW, you can escalate treatment with a steam cleaner per its instructions.

172

KNOW THE CODE

Much like how laundry garments have symbols to communicate washing and drying instructions, upholstery has its own cleaning language. Use the key below to understand what the care letters mean:

O Clean with cold water, because it's made from organic materials.

S Clean only with a solvent-based cleanser—such as denatured alcohol—or dry-clean. Do not use water or water-based products.

SW Clean with a solvent-based cleaner and/or water-based cleanser.

V Wash regularly with warm water and mild soap. Do not use harsh cleaning products.

W Clean with water or a water-based solvent or foam.

X Clean only with a vacuum, or hire a professional.

If the sofa has been reupholstered or you have lost its care instructions, test an inconspicuous area to see how water affects the fabric. Then clean according to the indications below.

173

ATTACK THE STAIN

The cleaning codes should be considered to determine whether to use a solvent-based or water-based cleaner when spot-treating a stain, and adapting them with the laundry-stain guide (see item 156) can yield a custom solution. Minimize the amount of liquid so it doesn't supersaturate the furniture, and always test on a small, inconspicuous area.

174

FRESHEN UP

Baking soda is the go-to method for freshening upholstery. Using a cheese shaker, sprinkle a thin layer of baking soda over cushions and upholstered surfaces. Let it sit for at least 15 minutes or overnight, vacuum clean, and the stale smell will disappear.

175

SHAMPOO UPHOLSTERY

Unless your upholstery is coded S or X and is not water tolerant, a simple shampoo can help lift out unsightly marks.

SUDS Create a foam by whipping up equal parts dishwashing liquid and water. Apply the foam to the stain.

RUB Gently work the foam into the stain with your fingertips so as not to strain the fabric. Let it sit for 5 minutes.

REMOVE Rinse a sponge with water and apply water to the stain to remove the soapy foam. Blot dry with a microfiber cloth. You may have to repeat on stubborn stains.

DRY Soak up as much moisture as you can with a microfiber cloth. Let air-dry completely.

176
CARE FOR FINE LEATHER

Leather ages over time and with use. It takes on an attractive patina, but still needs regular cleaning to keep it in top shape. When you turn your attention to leather furniture, be mindful of where it sits in your room: Keep it out of direct sunlight and away from vents, both of which will dry and weaken the leather.

STEP ONE Clean as you did according to the entry for nonleather upholstery (see item 171), vacuuming dust and dirt and running a lint roller over any remaining pet hair.

STEP TWO Wipe it down with a dry microfiber cloth. Fill a bucket with equal parts white vinegar and water. Wet a microfiber cloth so it's damp but not saturated. Wipe the leather sofa cushions and body, repeatedly rinsing the cloth and dipping it in the cleaning solution.

STEP THREE Dry the leather with a clean cloth—water that sits on the leather will stain and weaken the upholstery.

177
TREAT STAINS ON LEATHER

Leather furniture is expensive, so it can be scary when you notice marks on the upholstery. Follow these guidelines to help put yourself at ease.

GREASE Sprinkle baking soda on the stained area. Let it sit for a few hours, then brush it off with a clean rag.

INK Dip a cotton swab in rubbing alcohol and dab the swab on the ink stain. Make sure to lightly apply the alcohol to minimize the ink spreading.

DARK SPOTS ON LIGHT LEATHER Make a paste of equal parts cream of tartar and lemon juice. Apply paste to the spot and leave on for 10 minutes, then wipe the leather with a damp cloth and let air-dry.

179
DUST WOOD OFTEN

Wooden pieces manufactured in the past 50 years have a hard, clean finish that protects the surface and maintains sheen. Resist applying commercial polishes that can damage the factory finish. The best care you can give your wood furniture is to actually do as little as possible. Wipe their surfaces weekly with a barely damp microfiber cloth to pick up dust, and leave it at that.

178
OPT FOR A NATURAL POLISH

Commercial furniture polishes contain chemicals that aren't good choices for use in our homes. They're not good for recently manufactured furniture, either; they will dim—and can damage—the factory finish. Use the Furniture Polish (see item 197) to create a lustrous shine that doesn't feel oily. Once a month, dip a corner of a microfiber cloth in the polish and rub it on with a brisk circular motion, then buff with a dry microfiber cloth.

180
GO BEYOND DUSTING

Wooden coffee tables and end tables may accumulate more than dust over time and need an occasional cleaning. Put 1 Tbsp. Castile soap into 1 qt. water, wet a microfiber cloth or soft sponge, and squeeze most of the moisture out before washing the surface. Follow with a second, clean damp cloth to remove any soap residue. Dry to avoid water spots and streaks.

181
TEND TO YOUR FIREPLACE

Deep-clean the fireplace at least twice per year, and clean out the ashes weekly while in use. It's also important to have it inspected and professionally cleaned once a year—for recommendations, check the website for the Chimney Safety Institute of America.

183
GET THE TOOLS

Cleaning the fireplace is a dirty job, and you'll need the right supplies to do a thorough job. Grab a drop cloth, gloves, a breathing mask, goggles, a scrub brush, rags, the vacuum, and microfiber cloths.

182
CLEAN THE FIREBOX

It takes three days for embers to completely cool, so if embers remain, wait at least that long after you have a fire to start cleaning. Avoid extinguishing a fire by dowsing with water, because it will produce a lot of smoke and make ash hard.

CLEAR Remove everything from the fireplace: the fireplace screen and cover, tools, grate, andirons/chenets, and unburned logs if you have them. Open the flue.

SPREAD Put wet coffee grounds on top of the fireplace ashes to prevent the ashes from flying into the air when you clean them out of the fireplace.

REMOVE Shovel and sweep the ashes together and put them in a sturdy bag or tin, preferably with a lid so they don't spread dust into the air. Sweep everywhere—top, bottom, back, and sides. Move ashes onto your compost pile outside.

VACUUM Use the dust-brush attachment to vacuum the interior top, bottom, back, sides, and the damper ledge, as well as the exterior of the fireplace and surround. Periodically clean the dust-brush attachment so that you don't transfer soot from one area to another. Clean the dust brush again when finished.

LOOSEN If the firebox is relatively new and doesn't have a thick coating of soot, spraying with the All-Purpose Cleaner (see item 197) will loosen it. Scrub the interior with a stiff brush, rinsing the brush in water when needed, then use a rag to wipe up the grime.

CUSTOMIZE Identify the material of your firebox, and follow the appropriate directions in item 184.

184
DEEP-CLEAN FIREBOXES

Whether you have a built-in masonry fireplace or a factory-built fireplace, regular seasonal cleaning will keep them beautiful and ready for the next chilly evening.

BRICK The firebox in traditional, built-in masonry fireplaces is lined with firebrick, which can withstand high temperatures. Cleaning it is a messy job but one you an do yourself. Cover the surrounding floor and furniture with drop cloths, and use a dust mask and work gloves.

Mix one part salt to one part mild dishwashing liquid or castile soap. Add just enough water to make a thick paste, and apply the paste to the wall with your hands. Let the paste sit for 10–15 minutes and scrub with a stiff-bristled brush. Remove residue with a wet sponge, rinsing it often, and repeat the process as necessary.

METAL AND CERAMIC Factory-built fireplaces use metal and ceramic liners in the firebox that are less likely to accumulate soot and easier to clean. Your vacuum's dust-brush attachment will usually remove any soot or dirt. Follow with soap and water if needed.

You should also hire a professional chimney sweep to clear the creosote from the chimney after each fire-burning season.

185
CLEAN A GAS FIREPLACE

Although gas fireplaces do not leave the ash of their wood-burning cousins, they still create a bit of soot from particles in the air. Follow these directions to maintain a tidy appearance.

STEP ONE Turn off the gas valve and wait for the firebox to cool.

STEP TWO Vacuum the firebox area, looking for dust, dirt, cobwebs, and anything else in the area. Check the valves, burners, and control area to be sure nothing could prevent its safe operation.

STEP THREE Vacuum in and around ceramic logs or any other items used to disperse the heat. If there are any small pieces like lava rocks, cover the attachment with cheesecloth or hosiery to prevent small pieces from getting sucked into the vacuum.

STEP FOUR Spray a clean microfiber cloth with the Glass Cleaner (see item 197) and wipe the interior of the screen. Use a new cloth and fresh spray to clean the exterior.

187
MIND THE MANTEL

Smoke and soot will inevitably darken your fireplace surround and mantel. It's a fairly easy process to clean, but knowing whether your material is sealed is important. To get started, clean everything off the mantel and take down any art hanging overhead. Keep the firebox-cleaning materials handy from item 183, and follow the appropriate directions for your surround.

STONE Dip a microfiber cloth or sponge in warm, soapy water and scrub. Rinse with a water-dampened cloth and thoroughly dry.

BRICK Follow the directions for cleaning brick in item 184.

WOOD Wipe with a warm, soapy solution on a microfiber cloth. Rinse with a clean, damp microfiber cloth. Make sure to thoroughly dry afterward, as standing water on wood will leave a mark.

METAL Spray the surface with the Nonabrasive Vinegar Cleaner (see item 197) and wipe with a microfiber cloth, always moving in the direction of the grain. Apply baby oil and wipe it off. Resistant stains can be cleaned with a baking soda paste, applied, and then rubbed off in the direction of the grain.

CONCRETE Dip a microfiber cloth or sponge in warm, soapy water and scrub. Rinse with a clean, damp cloth, then thoroughly dry. If the concrete is sealed, use a soft-bristled scrub brush.

TILE Dip a microfiber cloth or a sponge in warm, soapy water and scrub. Rinse with a clean, damp cloth and thoroughly dry. Clean grout with a grout brush and a paste of baking soda and hydrogen peroxide (see item 114).

186
REMEMBER THE ACCESSORIES

If it's too cold to clean the fireplace accessories outside, consider doing so in the bathtub. Just remember to lay a towel in the tub to protect the surface and another one on the floor to protect it.

LOOSEN Spray a microfiber cloth with the All-Purpose Cleaner (see item 197) and wipe the tools to eliminate the surface dirt and soot.

SOAK Lay a towel in the bathtub, move the fireplace accessories into the tub, and fill it with warm, soapy water.

CLEAN Scrub the accessories— mesh fireplace screen, andirons, chenets, grate—with a scrub brush, toothbrush, or microfiber cloth. Rinse and thoroughly dry.

188
WIPE FIREPLACE GLASS CLEAN

Vacuum the firebox-facing glass to remove any ashes or dirt. Spray a microfiber cloth with the Glass Cleaner (see item 197) and wipe the glass. This will require a little elbow grease and repeat sprays in order to break down the soot. Use a razor blade if you can't get a piece of dirt to come loose, and swap in a new cloth when one gets dirty. Do the same process on the front-facing side, which should be much easier!

189
CARE FOR YOUR ART

You may not have a Monet in your personal collection, but every painting or framed family photography collects dust, pet hair, or smoke residue over time. Whether they are valuable on the art market or valuable because they hold a sentimental memory, plan to seasonally clean with a light hand.

PAINTINGS ON CANVAS Oil and acrylic paintings on stretched canvas are never put behind glass, so they're exposed to household dust that settled on them. There's a great risk of accidental damage, so proceed with caution. Using only a soft sable brush such as an artist would use, delicately skim the surface of the canvas to get the dust off.

FRAMES Even brand-new frames often have delicate finishes that are easily scratched. Never put any polishing product, water, or soap on a frame. Dust gently with a dry microfiber cloth, wrapping it around your finger if needed to get into small spaces; rely on a cotton swab for still smaller areas in intricately carved frames.

MUSEUM GLASS A relatively new technological innovation, museum glass doesn't reflect any ambient light, appearing as though there is no glass and resulting in extraordinary clarity of the artwork. It's expensive, and you certainly don't want to damage it. Mix ¼ c. rubbing alcohol and ¼ c. water in a spray bottle. Spray onto a microfiber cloth; never spray toward the glass. Clean in circular motions

until all fingerprints, smudges, and spots are gone.

ACRYLIC OR PLEXIGLASS These lighter-weight alternatives to glass also have advantages of UV coatings and being able to withstand more shock without breaking. They are almost universally used in larger frames and in places where shattered glass could be dangerous, such as in children's rooms and in earthquake zones. The biggest drawback is that they are softer than glass and are easily scratched by even paper towels or a dry cloth. Spot-clean fingerprints with a dry microfiber cloth in circular motions. If something more is required, a mild soap-and-water solution may be more effective. Rinse with clear water and dry with a second cloth.

CLEAR GLASS This old standby costs less than acrylic and is still popular in frames smaller than 14 by 11 in. and will be found on vintage and antique art. This is the one and only time you might use the Glass Cleaner (see item 197) on framed art.

190
PRESERVE OLD FURNITURE

Inherited or acquired, your antique wood furniture requires a hands-off approach. If you've ever seen *The Antiques Roadshow*, you know that a bad cleaning or restoration can do permanent damage and reduce the value and marketability of your prized antique. Older furniture with an oiled finish does best with regular dusting only; never apply polish or wax. If the wood becomes dry, it needs to be re-oiled. If your antique already has a wax finish, it must be waxed again and energetically buffed every six months to keep its shine. Don't use soap or oil polishes on top of wax. With all antiques, take a little more care when dusting to prevent accidental damage.

Many museums have days devoted to assessing people's antiques and providing advice. If you're unsure how to maintain an ornate or valuable piece of furniture, check whether a museum has a conservation department or if a curator can refer you to a nearby expert in restoration and preservation.

Quick Tip

DON'T USE BREAD
Despite online advice to clean paintings with white bread (because dirt does adhere to it), avoid the temptation. The bread leaves food particles that will attract bugs and promote the growth of mold.

191
TAKE CARE OF YOUR TV

Whether you have weekly family movie night or binge-watch the latest hit, your television sees a lot of action. Give it the care it deserves, and dust it weekly to keep the picture sharp and the operation efficient. Before you get started, unplug the electronics, and wait until the television cools down.

CATHODE RAY TUBE TELEVISION The old type of TV with the clunky back still gets some use. To clean, spray a microfiber cloth with the Glass Cleaner (see item 197) and wipe the front and back clean. Dry with a clean microfiber cloth.

PLASMA, LCD, LED, REAR-PROJECTION SCREEN These screens are super sensitive, so dust them with a clean, dry microfiber cloth. Wipe down the front and back and buttons to prevent any dust from collecting. If the dust is resistant, dampen a clean microfiber cloth with distilled water and wipe the surface lightly in wide circles. If there are fingerprints or any stubborn goo, use a solution of one part distilled white vinegar to one part distilled water. Spray a microfiber cloth and wipe the spotted area, then let it air-dry.

192
DEEP-CLEAN YOUR SPEAKERS

Speakers tend to disappear into your living room, so it's natural to overlook them. Use the upholstery brush on a low setting to vacuum the fabric cover, and vacuum the back of the cover if its removable. Use a lint roller to collect any resistant dust. For any nonfabric areas of the speaker cabinet, dampen a clean microfiber cloth with water and wipe away any dust, then let the speakers air-dry.

193
TAKE CONTROL OF THE REMOTE

We've already emphasized cleaning the remote when you have a sick family member (see item 148), but it's a good tool to keep clean regardless!

STEP ONE Remove the batteries to avoid a shock or damaging the electronics.

STEP TWO Use a microfiber cloth dampened with a solution of one part alcohol to one part distilled water (or use a disposable wipe) to wipe the front, sides, and back of the remote.

STEP THREE Use a cotton swab dipped in the alcohol solution to reach between and on the sides of buttons.

STEP FOUR Let completely air-dry before replacing the batteries.

194
REVIEW YOUR BOOKS

Books are wonderful objects in the home and serve as conversation pieces and reference resources. But they also tend to sit untouched for years at a time. Give them some attention to eliminate common problems, and embrace the idea of editing your collection.

DUST Get rid of the dust on the exteriors of books by wiping with a microfiber cloth. The interior may require opening and a gentle shake to dislodge dust.

BUGS Little insects can make a meal of a book's paper and glue. If bugs have gotten to a book, tightly wrap it in plastic wrap and leave it in the freezer for a few hours to kill the bugs.

MILDEW If you notice mildew spores on the pages, sprinkle cornstarch inside the book and leave it for 1 day before removing.

SCENTS If the book smells musty, stand it up with its pages spread in a covered container with a fresh box of baking soda, and leave for a week.

195
CLEAN THE BOOKSHELVES

To clean bookshelves, first remove the books to have a clear working space. Vacuum the bookshelves using the crevice attachment to get into the corners and wipe clean with a damp microfiber cloth. For resistant dust, spray with the All-Purpose Cleaner (see item 197). Rinse with a damp cloth and air-dry.

196
FRESHEN YOUR PLANTS

Plants combat chemicals and other toxins in the area, as well as add life and color to a room. But plants also collect dust when they're kept indoors and miss Mother Nature's cleansing showers and breezes, so follow these guidelines to help keep them healthy.

HEARTY, WAXY LEAVES Hold each leaf in your hand for support to minimize damage, and gently wipe it with a damp microfiber cloth.

DELICATE LEAVES For plants with delicate leaves and good drainage, a gentle rinse in the sink or outside will do the trick.

CACTI AND SUCCULENTS For plants that are either delicate or sensitive to overwatering, mist your plants with water from a spray bottle.

Quick Tip

CURATE CAREFULLY

Make your family book sweep an annual event. Donate books that your children have outgrown (libraries love them for annual fund-raising sales) or trade them at used bookstores for store credit. Embrace the idea of curating your collection—being more selective about the books you keep elevates their significance!

197 CLEAN AND POLISH THE WHOLE HOME

Keep a batch of these natural cleaning products on hand to deal with accidents and maintain clean surfaces.

ALL-PURPOSE CLEANER

2 tsp. borax
¼ tsp. liquid castile soap
10 drops lemon essential oil

Mix all ingredients with hot water in a 16-oz. spray bottle.

FURNITURE POLISH

½ c. jojoba oil
2 Tbsp. distilled white vinegar
5 drops lemon essential oil for scent

Pour the jojoba oil, vinegar, and essential oil in a sealable 8-oz. jar. Vigorously shake to emulsify before using.

GLASS CLEANER

¼ c. distilled white vinegar
5 drops lemon essential oil

Mix all ingredients with hot water in a 16-oz. spray bottle.

NONABRASIVE VINEGAR CLEANER

1 part distilled white vinegar
2 parts water
5 drops lavender essential oil

Combine the vinegar and water in a 16-oz. spray bottle. Add 5 drops of essential oils if you don't like the smell of vinegar—my favorites are lavender, grapefruit, orange lemon, and peppermint.

LIVING ROOM
Checklists

To convey a welcoming atmosphere to both family and guests, keep clutter out and dust and dirt on the run. Depending on how much use it gets, the living room merits a daily pass through to guarantee that the space feels fresh. Pick up messes immediately and give it a thorough cleaning every week, so old magazines and tennis shoes under the ottoman don't become permanent.

Numbers refer to the general cleaning entries, so make sure to reference the appropriate supporting items to address specific materials and circumstances.

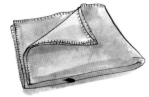

DAILY

- ☐ Quick pick-up
- ☐ Spot-clean spills and potential stains
- ☐ Sweep or vacuum floors *30*
- ☐ Straighten throw pillows
- ☐ _____
- ☐ _____
- ☐ _____

WEEKLY

- ☐ Dust window treatments *14*
- ☐ Dust doors and baseboards *18*
- ☐ Clean switch plates *19*
- ☐ Dust ceilings and walls *20*
- ☐ Vacuum carpets and area rugs *42, 44*
- ☐ Dust lampshades and chandeliers *52, 56*
- ☐ Dust surfaces and accessories *170*
- ☐ Wipe wooden furniture *179*
- ☐ Dust television *191*
- ☐ Clean remote controls *193*

MONTHLY

- ☐ Clean mirrors *13*
- ☐ Clean window treatments *14*
- ☐ Wash trash bins *28*
- ☐ Clean doorknobs *29*
- ☐ Vacuum upholstered furniture *171, 176*
- ☐ Clean leather upholstery *176*
- ☐ Polish wood furniture *178*
- ☐ Dust and clean speakers *192*
- ☐ Dust books and bookshelves *194, 195*
- ☐ _____

SEASONALLY (SPRING AND FALL)

- ☐ Wash windows *12*
- ☐ Deep-clean window treatments *14*
- ☐ Wipe doors and baseboards *18*
- ☐ Clean walls *20*
- ☐ Clean exterior doors *27*
- ☐ Deep-clean lampshades *53*
- ☐ Clean lamp bases *55*
- ☐ Clean sconces, chandeliers, and light fixtures *54, 56, 57*
- ☐ Deep-clean upholstery *171*
- ☐ Deep-clean fireplace *181*
- ☐ Clean framed art *189*
- ☐ Clean and vacuum bookshelves *195*
- ☐ Dust plants *196*
- ☐ Hire a chimney sweep *184*
- ☐ _____
- ☐ _____
- ☐ _____
- ☐ _____
- ☐ _____
- ☐ _____
- ☐ _____

198

EMBRACE THE DINING ROOM

For years, we've heard "The dining room is dead." It seems everyone wanted more relaxed, casual spaces for entertaining, so walls came down and the grand eat-in kitchen took over. But now people recognize the value of a devoted space for meals. It doesn't have to be formal or fussy, just special so that we can sit, dine, and converse.

Still, some dining rooms don't see traffic every day, so dust builds up. Mail collects. Piles accumulate. Panic ensues when you plan a party for a room that hasn't seen a cleaning in weeks. Do a quick weekly dusting and a more thorough monthly cleaning, and you'll always be company-ready. If you eat there nightly like we do, clean it daily so every dinner is a delight.

199

PREPARE FOR GUESTS

Plan a concentrated cleaning twice a year. Anticipate fall and winter holiday dinners, as well as spring religious holidays when you'll entertain extended family.

RUGS Vacuum the rug as well as the floor. If possible, take both rug and pad outside to air out. Shake out the dust, or if the rug is too large to shake, lay it pile side down and beat the back with a broom to dislodge dust and dirt. If your rug is simply too cumbersome to carry outside, move the dining room table to the side of the room, roll up the rug and pad, and clean the floor underneath.

FLOORS Take advantage of the floor being exposed to give it an extensive cleaning. See items 033–041 to be confident of the best method for your particular flooring.

WINDOW TREATMENTS Air out draperies, fabric shades, and blinds. Wash or dry-clean if necessary (see items 014–017).

WINDOWS Wash interior and exterior glass (see item 012).

CEILINGS AND WALLS Dust is redistributed throughout the house whenever the HVAC unit is heating or cooling, and leaves deposits on your ceiling and walls. See items 020–026 for the most efficient way to restore the true color and finish.

VENTS Wash floor vents in warm, soapy water to minimize dust buildup, and air-dry (see item 113).

LIGHT FIXTURES Take down ceiling fixtures and sconces for the easiest cleaning. Wash fabric and glass shades following the guidelines in items 051–055.

200

CHOOSE THE RIGHT LINENS

Cloth napkins, placemats, and table runners aren't just for company. Using them is more environmentally friendly than disposable paper products, and linen place settings can often be machine-washed. But perhaps the most compelling reason show they add intimacy and coziness to the dining room, making even Wednesday-night breakfast-for-dinners festive!

201

WASH TABLE LINENS RIGHT

Don't eschew cloth napkins for fear of complex washing—most new cloths can generally go in the washing machine. If there are any stains, identify the food or drink culprits and follow the instructions from item 156 to spot-treat them. After treating the specific stains, simply load the washing machine with similarly colored linens without overfilling. Wash on the gentle cycle with warm water and select a cold after-rinse.

Quick Tip

SOFTEN CLOTHS NATURALLY

Commercial fabric softeners weaken fibers and, because table linens need frequent washing, shouldn't be used on them. For a natural fabric softener, put ½ c. white vinegar in the washing machine's fabric softener dispenser so it's added during the rinse cycle.

202
HAND-WASH HEIRLOOMS

Older linen cloths, heirlooms, and antiques benefit from hand-washing. If you're just too tired, you can leave them to soak overnight in clean water.

STEP ONE Line the sink (or a large container) with a towel to facilitate lifting the wet linens from the sink later. Fill with ice water and submerge linen napkins and tablecloths.

STEP TWO Grab the four corners of the towel lining the sink and lift the towel, pulling all the linens out of the water along with it. Drain the ice water, and lower the towel-wrapped linens back into the sink.

STEP THREE Spot-treat any stains according to the stain guidelines (see item 156). Refill the sink with warm water and the Laundry Detergent (see item 157) and return the linens.

STEP FOUR Carefully agitate the linens in the water (avoiding the temptation to rub or wring linens), then let the linens sit in the soapy water for 15–30 minutes. Don't leave linens overnight in soapy water!

STEP FIVE Lift the linens out of the water again using the towel, and drain the sink. Rinse the soap out until water runs clear.

STEP SIX Gently squeeze out excess water and roll the linens in dry towels, squeezing to release more water. Whenever it's practical, line-dry linens. If they're white, put them in the sun; dry colors in the shade. Take them down and iron them while they're still damp.

203
IRON WHILE DAMP

Previous generations sprayed clean clothes with water and then rolled them up until it was time to iron. They did this because it's easier to remove wrinkles in cotton and linen when they are slightly damp. Now you can just take them out of the dryer a little early and skip the extra step.

205 PAD THE SURFACE

Put a thick white towel over the ironing board when ironing napkins and cloths. It helps grip the fabric and smooth out wrinkles as you go. To avoid the shine that sometimes appears, iron tablecloths from the reverse side.

Place monograms and other embroidery face down into a plush towel and also iron from the back to help prevent flattening the stitches.

206
HANG THE LINENS

Save cardboard tubes from gift-wrapping or shelf-paper rolls and cut a slit down one side. Slide each one over the bottom of a coat hanger and hang a linen over it. Consider a layer of acid-free tissue between the cardboard and the cloth. You'll need to fold the cloth in to fit the hanger, but the tube will help prevent a hard crease resulting from the hanger and the need to iron again. Alternatively, use a skirt hanger with clips to store linens.

204
MAKE ROOM FOR IRONING

Wrestling with a large tablecloth over an ironing board can be frustrating. Consider covering your bedroom floor with a clean sheet, with the board between the sheet and your bed. Place the wrinkled, damp tablecloth on top of the sheet and start ironing the tablecloth, moving the pressed area onto the bed as you go. The sheet will keep the damp tablecloth from picking up dirt, and elevating the ironed section will minimize new creases and large wrinkles after ironing.

Quick Tip

PRESERVE AND PROTECT

Tissue paper, newsprint, cardboard, wood, and even dry cleaning bags can damage linen and cotton. Vintage linens that have yellowed with thin spots illustrate the results of improper storage. Invest in buffered acid-free tissue to preserve fine linens. Whether you are hanging, rolling, or folding your linens, put a layer of acid-free tissue beneath the linen; incorporate it with the cloth or napkin as you fold or roll. If you're storing linens on wooden shelves, line the shelves with a double layer of acid-free tissue.

207 TREAT DINING ROOM STAINS

When entertaining guests, the best advice for handling a stain is to act quickly to improve your chances of removing it without panicking and causing embarrassment. If someone spills a glass of red wine, just blot away as much as possible, generously sprinkle with table salt, cover with a napkin, and attend to it as soon as guests have left.

DRINK RINGS	
FINISHED WOOD	Apply petroleum jelly or mayonnaise to the ring, and let it sit for 8–10 hours before wiping with a microfiber cloth.
UNSEALED WOOD	Buff the stain out of the wood with light sandpaper.
MARBLE	Make a paste of baking soda and water, apply the paste, and cover with plastic wrap for 24 hours. Rinse, dry, and buff.
LINENS (TEA OR COFFEE)	Blot any excess moisture, then apply lemon juice or white vinegar and leave for 5–10 minutes. Work dishwashing liquid into the stain, and rinse.
LINENS (RED WINE)	Generously apply table salt and leave for 1 hour, remove the salt, then pour boiling water through the stain. Repeat as needed.

WINE	
FINISHED WOOD	Blot immediately. Apply a paste of equal parts baking soda and either lemon oil or linseed oil. Leave for 30 minutes, wipe off with damp microfiber cloth, and dry with a clean cloth.
MARBLE	Blot immediately. Apply a paste of equal parts baking soda and water, then cover with plastic wrap for 24 hours. Rinse, dry, and buff.
LINENS	Generously apply table salt and leave for 1 hour, remove the salt, then pour boiling water through the stain. Repeat as needed.

CANDLE WAX	
FINISHED WOOD	Apply a freezer pack or ice cubes in a plastic bag to harden wax, then gently scrape away with an expired credit card at a 45-degree angle. Treat with the Furniture Polish (see item 197) and buff with a microfiber cloth.
UNSEALED WOOD	Apply a freezer pack or ice cubes in a plastic bag to harden wax, then gently scrape away with an expired credit card at a 45-degree angle. If wax has seeped in, cover the spot with layers of paper towels and hold an iron on its lowest setting—with no steam—over the towels to melt the wax and transfer it to the towels.
MARBLE	Apply a freezer pack or ice cubes in a plastic bag to harden wax, then gently scrape away with an expired credit card at a 45-degree angle. Use warm, soapy water to remove wax residue, then rinse and buff.
GLASS	Gently scrape away with an expired credit card at a 45-degree angle. Warm remaining wax with a hair dryer and scrape. Clean with the Glass Cleaner (see item 197).
LINENS	Put linens in a large plastic bag, then into the freezer, to harden the wax. Follow instructions for removing wax from unsealed wood. Flush the spot with rubbing alcohol if there's any tint from colored wax.

208
CARE FOR FINE CHINA

Whether you have a newly crafted set or your grandmother's gold-edged heirlooms from Europe, delicate porcelain dinnerware brings a sense of elegance to any meal. Preserve this elegance, and resist the urge to put china in the dishwasher and risk any chips or fading of intricate designs.

REMOVE Scrape food with a rubber spatula—avoiding metal utensils that may cause damage—then rinse.

PROTECT Line your sink with a towel or a rubber mat to prevent accidental chipping or breaking if a plate drops.

WASH Fill the sink with warm water and a few squirts of mild dishwashing liquid, then use a soft cloth or sponge to clean each piece. Rinse, then dry with a clean microfiber cloth.

209
STORE IT SAFELY

Put a paper towel, coffee filter, felt, or flannel cloth between each plate and store in stacks of no more than five. Such liners will prevent cracking and chipping and stress on plates. Never stack china cups; instead, hang them from specially installed hooks or stand them on a shelf base down to protect the rim.

210
CARE FOR CRYSTAL AND GLASS

When washing fragile crystal and glass, line your sink with a towel or a rubber mat to help prevent chipping or breaking. Add 1 Tbsp. distilled white vinegar to your rinse water to prevent water spots on the glass. Store glasses rim up if you use them frequently and rim down if you seldom entertain.

211
ENJOY YOUR SILVER

It's tempting to save your cherished silver for special events only. But using and cleaning your silver every day is the best way to prevent tarnish.

DISHWASHER You can usually wash your sterling silver in the dishwasher as long as you separate it from the stainless flatware—stainless steel will chemically react with silver and permanently stain it. But make sure to remove silver before the dry cycle and instead dry it with a clean, dry towel.

HAND-WASH If you prefer to wash silver flatware by hand, try using a microfiber cloth and mild dishwashing liquid. Silver is soft and can be easily scratched. Don't dump it into a pile in the sink! Thoroughly dry and buff with a clean, dry towel.

SPECIALTY Silver flatware with horn, ebony, or mother-of-pearl handles should not go in the dishwasher. Hand-wash, dry, and shine the handles with olive oil.

212
SHINE SILVERWARE

Regularly polish silver to prevent tarnish and corrosion. If it's correctly stored—in flannel cloths or felt—you buy yourself more time between cleanings. There are plenty of silver polishes on the market, but they give off toxic fumes and require ventilation when polishing. My solution is fast and easy.

STEP ONE Line the kitchen sink or a large roasting pan with aluminum foil, shiny side up, and carefully lay silver pieces on top of the foil to avoid scratching the soft metal. If you use an aluminum pot, there's no need for foil.

STEP TWO Add ½ c.–1 c. baking soda, distributing over and around the silver, then pour boiling water into the pot, completely submerging all the pieces.

STEP THREE Leave for 5 minutes—no longer than 10 minutes!—and rinse with warm water. Dry, then buff with a microfiber cloth. If tarnish remains, repeat soaking for 5 minutes.

STEP FOUR Apply a plain toothpaste (not a gel or paste with whitening chemicals) to the tarnished areas with a microfiber cloth. Wipe off and buff.

213
MAINTAIN THE TABLE

The dining table is the centerpiece of the room, so make sure you give it your complete attention. It doesn't take much effort to maintain a wooden table, yet a little neglect quickly degrades its presence.

CLEAR FINISH If your wooden dining set has a hard, transparent finish common to manufactured wood furniture, it needs just a light dusting with a barely damp microfiber cloth. Wipe the legs in addition to the tabletop, especially in carved crevices where dust can settle. And note that I wrote *set*—don't forget wooden chairs in addition to your table!

PAINTED FURNITURE For painted furniture, clean with a damp cloth. When stains and spills occur, use mild, soapy water and immediately dry.

214
POLISH WOOD NATURALLY

Commercial furniture polishes were de rigueur in the 1950s, producing a shine that would guarantee social acceptance. Today we're aware that those products contain chemicals that aren't good choices for use in our homes, even if they infuse our dining room tables with a lemony scent. Despite the advertising message that magic comes from an aerosol can, you can protect your wood furniture and buff it to a shine with all-natural cleaning materials.

The Furniture Polish (see item 197) contains only natural ingredients, which I prefer to use in my house. It's safer than toxic commercial polishes and produces a lovely sheen. Dip a corner of a microfiber cloth in the polish and rub it on with a brisk circular motion, then buff with a dry microfiber cloth. To avoid buildup, I polish only once a month or when the wood begins to look and feel dry.

215
ENTERTAIN WITH EASE

Having a meal with friends and family is one of the great joys in life, but it's easy for a simple gathering to spiral out of control with elaborate plans and good intentions. Remember, your guests are here to spend time with you, and no one will enjoy themselves if you're too overwhelmed to share the experience. Welcome them into your home and take pleasure in their company so you'll be energized and want to do it again!

216
JUST SAY YES

When someone offers to help clear the table, be gracious and take them up on their offer. If a friend helps put dishes in the sink while you make coffee or serve dessert, your spouse can remain seated to entertain the other guests or vice versa.

217
PREP IN ADVANCE

Make-ahead dishes are entertaining lifesavers, and cleaning in advance is just as valuable. Dusting and vacuuming the dining room can be done a day early, and no one will notice a day's worth of foot traffic. You can set the table the day before, too. Doing as much as you can leading up to a dinner party saves you stress on the big day, and a beautifully set table instills a festive mood while you focus on to the menu.

218 CLEAN AS YOU GO

You know that guests will congregate in the kitchen—the mouthwatering scents and your presence as host are irresistible! Your guests will enjoy seeing your culinary efforts, but not a messy, chaotic room. Load utensils and bowls into the dishwasher as you finish with them, and wash and dry pots and pans and put them away as time permits. And keep a microfiber cloth accessible to quickly wipe spills on your countertops.

Quick Tip

MIX IT UP

Changes in temperature and humidity can hurt wood furniture, so regularly rearrange the room to minimize the time one piece sits in adverse conditions. Avoid strong sunlight and heating sources such as radiators, space heaters, and fireplaces.

DINING ROOM
Checklists

The dining room is spare enough that an errant cobweb or a dusty tabletop scream, "I'm not ready!" So hold on to this checklist, and always keep your dining room presentable for guests.

Numbers refer to the general cleaning entries, so make sure to reference the appropriate supporting items to address specific materials and circumstances.

DAILY

- ☐ Spot-clean spills and potential stains
- ☐ Sweep or vacuum floors *30*
- ☐ Spot-clean table linens *156*
- ☐ Wash table linens *201*
- ☐ Clear table of clutter *198*
- ☐ Wipe dining room table *213*
- ☐ _____

WEEKLY

- ☐ Dust window treatments *14*
- ☐ Dust doors and baseboards *18*
- ☐ Clean switch plates *19*
- ☐ Dust ceilings and walls *20*
- ☐ Mop floors *31*
- ☐ Vacuum carpets and area rugs *42, 44*
- ☐ Dust sconces, lampshades and chandeliers *52, 54, 56*
- ☐ _____
- ☐ _____
- ☐ _____
- ☐ _____
- ☐ _____
- ☐ _____
- ☐ _____

MONTHLY

- ☐ Clean mirrors *13*
- ☐ Clean window treatments *14*
- ☐ Clean doorknobs *29*
- ☐ Polish wood furniture *214*
- ☐ Clean sconces, chandeliers, and light fixtures *52, 54, 56*
- ☐ _____
- ☐ _____

SEASONALLY (SPRING AND FALL)

- ☐ Wash windows *12*
- ☐ Deep-clean window treatments *14*
- ☐ Wipe doors and baseboards *18*
- ☐ Clean walls *20*
- ☐ Deep-clean lampshades *53*
- ☐ Clean lamp bases *55*
- ☐ Clean sconces, chandeliers, and light fixtures *54, 56, 57*
- ☐ Polish silver *212*
- ☐ Deep-clean carpet and pad *199*
- ☐ Clean underneath rugs *199*
- ☐ Wash floor vents *199*
- ☐ _____
- ☐ _____
- ☐ _____
- ☐ _____
- ☐ _____
- ☐ _____
- ☐ _____
- ☐ _____

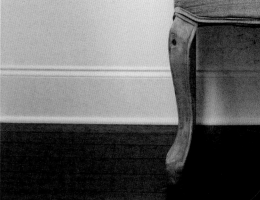

219
CREATE A SANCTUARY

Some cleaning habits are second nature by the time you're an adult: making the bed every day, putting dirty clothes in the hamper, returning the clothes you tried on and decided not to wear to the closet. It's tempting to leave one of those tasks undone when pressed for time. After all, only your nearest and dearest will see. But a clean and uncluttered bedroom is essential to creating a relaxing space where you can retreat. Take care of yourself by fostering a sanctuary in this intimate space.

222
PROTECT PILLOWS

A zippered pillow protector fits snugly over the pillow; the pillowcase goes on top of it. This extra layer prevents natural skin oil and lotions from staining the pillow, extending its useful life. But more important, a cover protects your family from dust mites and other allergens inside the pillow. Wash it monthly as you would a pillowcase, without bleach or fabric softener. Put it in the dryer on a low-heat setting, but do not iron.

220
TAKE IT EASY

Because the bedroom is not on show for guests, it's sometimes the last place we decorate. If that's the case with you, rethink your priorities. We spend one-third of our lives in the bed, sleeping to rejuvenate our bodies. Make your bedroom a spot that rejuvenates your spirit, too, giving you a boost to start the day and calming you in the evening. But consider long-term-care commitments and less time-consuming alternatives—when the room is quick and easy to clean, you can spend your time on more important things.

WINDOW COVERINGS Instead of silk draperies, consider the attractive options in easy-to-clean indoor/outdoor fabric or no drapes at all. Plantation shutters are stylish and easy to clean.

FLOORS Do you really need carpeting, or would hardwood floors allow you to capture more of the dust that's hiding in your room?

BEDDING Look for bed skirts, decorative pillows, and duvet covers in washable fabrics. I gravitate toward white bedding because it looks great and tossing it in the wash once a week keeps it clean.

221
LAUNDER SHEETS WEEKLY

I prefer to wash our sheets once a week. It doesn't take much time, and the payoff comes when I slide into a fresh, spotless cocoon at night. Some things about washing sheets are second nature by now—use warm water, wash colors separately, and use a low-heat drying cycle. I've learned that the dryer heat will permanently set a stain, so make sure to treat all stains (see item 156) before bed linens go into the dryer.

224
CASE OUT PILLOWS

It's a good idea to have extra pillowcases on hand in case they need laundering more than once a week. Makeup and face lotions often soil a pillowcase. Replace it right away and treat the stain. If you have a teen in the house, it's a good idea to give her or him a fresh pillowcase frequently to stave off acne breakouts.

225
MINIMIZE WRINKLES

Take sheets out of the dryer before they are completely dry and you'll have fewer wrinkles. Make the bed, smoothing out wrinkles with your hand, and let the sheets finish air-drying before you put a cover over them.

223
SOFTEN BEDDING

Instead of using commercial fabric softeners that include harmful chemicals, simply pour ½ c. white vinegar in the fabric softener dispenser with each wash. Vinegar is a natural softening agent and removes soap residue from the sheets.

226
CARE FOR PILLOWS

You may regularly wash your pillowcases, but what about the pillows themselves? Bedroom pillows need a thorough wash twice a year. Most synthetic and down pillows are machine washable, but double-check the care tag.

STEP ONE Strip off any cases, sham covers, protectors, and allergy covers, and wash those separately.

STEP TWO Wash two pillows at a time to balance the load in the machine, using liquid detergent and warm water. Program the machine to go through two rinse cycles to remove as much soap as possible.

STEP THREE Transfer pillows to the dryer and set it on the air cycle for down or a low-heat setting for synthetics. Add a couple of wool dryer balls to fluff the pillows, separate the down, and deter clumps.

227
REVITALIZE MEMORY FOAM

Pillows made from memory foam are becoming increasingly popular due to their ability to create a customized fit while still providing support. But this material requires special care.

DUNK Remove the cover from the pillow and submerge it in a sink or tub filled with warm water.

MIX Add 1 Tbsp. mild liquid laundry detergent to the water, and swirl and squeeze the pillow to let the water and soap work their way through.

RINSE Drain the soapy water and refill the sink with clean, cool water. Swirl and squeeze the pillow— replacing the water as necessary— until you are confident there is no more soap in the pillow.

DRY Never put memory foam in the dryer. Instead, gently press water out and allow it to completely air-dry on a white towel.

228
SHIELD YOUR COMFORTER

Don't wash a comforter more often than twice a year. Washing too frequently will compact the fill, diminishing its capacity for warmth. It's the air trapped within a light, fluffy filling that provides the insulation to keep your body heat from escaping into the room. Protect the comforter from body oils by encasing it in fabric. An attractive duvet cover can be washed monthly, saving the comforter for a seasonal cleaning.

229
CLEAN THE COMFORTER

Before you wash a comforter or duvet, read the care tag attached to one of the corners and follow the directions. Check for stains, tears, and holes that need repair. Spot-clean according to the guidelines in the laundry-stains list (see item 156), but push the filling aside when treating stains. And consider your washer's capacity for a king- or queen-size comforter; you may need to go to a laundromat for larger-capacity washers, or to a dry cleaner.

DOWN, COTTON, OR SYNTHETIC Wash comforters filled with these materials on the delicate cycle with warm or cold water and a mild detergent. Distribute the comforter evenly in the machine and use an extra rinse cycle. Dry on the fluff setting with wool dryer balls, and periodically stop the dryer to fluff and distribute the filler. You could also air-dry the comforter, fluffing and distributing the fill as it dries.

WOOL Hand-wash wool-filled comforters. Fill the bathtub with warm, soapy water and gently press the comforter up and down in the water. Rinse thoroughly, repeating until the water runs clear. Gently press excess water from the comforter and hang outside to dry. Before hand-washing, consider the risk of felting and the weight when wet. You may prefer to dry-clean it.

SILK There's really no way around it: A silk-filled comforter must be dry-cleaned to avoid damage.

230
FRESHEN A MATTRESS

Even though you can't wash your mattress, you can regularly clean it. And you should. Follow the suggestions below to make it more comfortable for sleep and to help it last as long as possible.

STEP ONE Strip the bed and let the mattress air out for an hour or two.

STEP TWO Vacuum the mattress with the upholstery and crevice attachment. Be meticulous about covering the entire surface and getting into the seams: the vacuum will suction up dust mites if you're thorough.

STEP THREE Spot-clean stains, adapting guidelines for removing laundry stains (see item 156) when appropriate. When in doubt, follow the directions for cleaning upholstery (see item 172). Be careful not to saturate the mattress, and let it completely air-dry.

STEP FOUR Deodorize the mattress by shaking an entire box of baking soda out over its surface. Let the baking soda sit for as long as you can to let it neutralize all odors, and then vacuum it up. The best time for you to freshen up your mattress is before you leave for vacation.

231
WASH THE MATTRESS PAD

Use a mattress pad to prolong the life of your mattress by screening it from accidental spills and from natural skin oils and perspiration that would otherwise yellow the mattress. If there's no care tag, follow these general directions.

COTTON Spot-treat stains first, machine-wash with warm water, and dry on a low-heat setting.

FOAM Because a washing machine is too hard on foam mattress pads, spot-clean instead if you see a stain. Otherwise, just vacuum both sides. If you feel that an overall cleaning is warranted, make a spray of one part mild soap to two parts water and spray it on the pad. Let it sit for 30 minutes, then thoroughly rinse in the shower or tub. Gently squeeze out the water and air-dry, flipping the pad as needed to completely dry.

VINYL AND PLASTIC Spot-clean any stains and vacuum the front and back. Put the pad in the washer with warm or cold water with mild detergent. Dry on the air-fluff cycle only, adding wool dryer balls to speed drying. If it is not completely dry when the cycle ends, leave it out to air-dry with the vinyl or plastic side up first, then turn it over to dry the fabric side.

EGG CRATE Spot-clean and vacuum both sides, then spray with a one part mild soap to two parts water. Rinse in a tub or shower and carefully squeeze out excess water so as not to rip the egg crate. Air-dry, flipping the pad as needed to dry it completely.

232

TREAT CURTAINS AND BED SKIRTS

In addition to the necessary bed fittings, you may enjoy dressing your bed with a bed skirt, decorative pillows, or bed curtains. All of these enhance the bed but are harder to categorize by cleaning methods. Read the attached care tag for special handling, but follow these general care instructions.

BED SKIRTS Silk and wool skirts must be dry-cleaned, but cotton and linen skirts can be machine-washed, particularly if they are white. With colors or patterns, check for colorfastness by wetting a small, inconspicuous corner and patting the spot with a white cotton washcloth to look for color bleeding. If there is none, machine-wash in cold water. If the color bleeds, dry-clean it. Dry on a medium or low heat setting, remove while still damp, and immediately iron.

DECORATIVE PILLOWS Pillows with beading and embroidery, especially on velvet, accumulate dust over time. Your best bet may be canned air, which is sold at photo-supply shops and used to clean dust off of camera lenses. Start in an area without beading or heavy embroidery to be certain the air pressure won't push the beads off. You can also try vacuuming on low suction, but first stretch hosiery over the dust-brush attachment to prevent snagging of any threads.

BED CURTAINS Treat curtains and canopies as you would window draperies, taking them down seasonally for cleaning (see item 017). If they are silk, wool, or lined draperies, dry cleaning is safer.

233

SCENT WITH LAVENDER

Using lavender essential oil is an indispensable part of my bedtime routine. Not only do I dab it onto my neck and wrists, but I also mist it over my pillow and linens. It's easy to make and creates a calming atmosphere.

LAVENDER ROOM SPRAY

1.5 oz. rubbing alcohol
1.5 oz. water
30 drops lavender essential oil

Pour the rubbing alcohol, water, and lavender essential oil into a 4-oz. spray bottle. Shake well before each use.

234

MAKE THE BED

A well-made bed, with edges tucked, surfaces smoothed, and pillows fluffed, is an inviting sight.

STEP ONE Place the pad over the mattress and pull the elastic restraints under the corners to hold it in place, then put the fitted sheet over the pad and mattress, pulling the elastic edges over the corners tightly.

STEP TWO If you use a flat sheet, lay it on the fitted sheet (patterned or finished side down). Align the top with the mattress, and drape at equal lengths on either side of the bed.

STEP THREE If you use a blanket, lay it over the flat sheet so the top falls about 5 inches below the top of the flat sheet and the sides fall at equal lengths on each side of the mattress.

STEP FOUR Tuck the blanket and sheet in at the bottom, and then fold hospital corners at the bottom. At the top, fold the sheet back.

STEP FIVE Lay a coverlet, duvet, or comforter atop the sheet or blanket. If you're using pillow shams, put them on pillows and stand them against the headboard. Put protective pillow covers and then pillowcases on the pillows and lean them horizontally in front of the shams or headboard. If you don't use extra pillows with shams, you can lay the pillows flat.

235

DON'T FORGET THE BEDFRAME

We're so good about cleaning sheets and pillowcases, but the frame—be it a wood tester, an upholstered headboard, a metal canopy, or a modern platform—gets taken for granted. Dust monthly with a damp microfiber cloth to avoid buildup.

236
ADDRESS THE DRESSER

Drawers may store clean clothes, but they still need to be seasonally cleaned and decluttered. Empty drawers and cabinets so you can thoroughly vacuum all interior spaces with a dust-brush attachment, then wipe with a soft cloth or sponge dampened with the All-Purpose Cleaner (see item 197), using a toothbrush to loosen debris around the edges and corners. Wipe again with a cloth dampened with water to remove any trace of the cleaner, then let them completely dry before returning the contents.

237
TACKLE A CEILING FAN

Clean fans twice a year, spreading a drop cloth or large sheet on the floor first and wearing safety glasses to protect your eyes from falling dust. It's easier to reach all the parts using a ladder, although you may be able to do so with a microfiber wand. Spray the All-Purpose Cleaner (see item 197) on a microfiber cloth or wand, and wipe each blade, top and bottom. Dust the motor housing as well as the downrod. Chances are you'll need to rinse the cloth and reapply spray or replace cloths as they become too dirty to pick up more dust.

238
CLEAN A FABRIC HEADBOARD

The best way to remove spots on a fabric headboard is with a little dish soap, although it's essential that you test the method on a discreet spot, especially if the fabric is decorative and may not be colorfast. A good testing spot is on the back of the headboard or at a level low enough not to show above the mattress.

SUDS Create a thick sudsy foam by whipping up equal parts dishwashing liquid and water. Apply the foam to the spot or stain.

RUB Gently work the foam into the stain with your fingertips so as not to strain the fabric. Let it sit for 5 minutes.

REMOVE Rinse a sponge with water and apply water to the stain to remove the soapy foam. Blot it dry with a microfiber cloth. You may have to repeat on stubborn stains.

DRY Soak up as much moisture as you can with a microfiber cloth. Let air-dry completely.

239
MAINTAIN A HUMIDIFIER

It's important to change the water every day and regularly inspect the unit. Mold and mildew are always a concern with a humidifier, so clean and disinfect it once a week. Refer to the owner's manual for cleaning instructions specific to your device, but otherwise follow these general guidelines to keep a clean machine.

STEP ONE Drain all water from the tank. Refill it with cold water and add 1 tsp. vinegar per gallon of water. Let it soak for 30 minutes while the vinegar kills mold and bacteria.

STEP TWO Take the machine apart to access the filter, water reservoir, and any other removable parts. Thoroughly rinse the filter with nothing but cold water; vinegar and soap may damage a filter.

STEP THREE Pour white vinegar into the water reservoir in the base of the unit, right up to the fill line, and let it soak for 30 minutes. Put other loose parts into a bowl or bucket of white vinegar for 30 minutes.

STEP FOUR Scrub the base and all loose parts—except for the filter—with a toothbrush, or any tool that came with the humidifier. Pay attention to mineral deposits and discolored areas. Drain the vinegar, rinse all parts, and let them air-dry.

STEP FIVE Reassemble your humidifier and then refill the tank with clean water. Remember: It's important to change the water in the tank every day.

240
HUNT FOR BUNNIES

Dust bunnies live in spots that we don't see regularly, so you'll need to seek them out. Under the bed is one of their favorite hiding places. Make a habit of using your microfiber wand to sweep under the bed, bedside table, and chest of drawers once a week.

241
CLEAN CLOSETS

An annual scrubbing of closets is crucial. They're dark and often crowded with lots of places for dust bunnies, cobwebs, and critters to hide. Take everything out of the closet—down to the bare walls and floors—and vacuum the floors, walls, and ceiling using the crevice and brush attachments to get into corners and high spots. Wash every surface and corner with the Nonabrasive Vinegar Cleaner (see item 197), which will not only loosen dirt but also kill moth eggs so small that you can't see them. Let the space air-dry before returning clothes, shoes, and boxes to the closet.

242
MAKE LAVENDER SACHETS

Lavender is a natural moth repellent, so lavender sachets are the perfect natural alternative to toxic moth balls. Not only are they simple to make, they also look and smell lovely. Follow these steps to create two sachets that you can place in your closet or tuck into drawers.

STEP ONE Cut a vintage handkerchief into four even squares, and sew two pieces of the fabric together, inside out, leaving a couple of inches at the top.

STEP TWO Flip the fabric right side out and fill sachets half full with dried lavender buds.

STEP THREE Carefully sew the remaining end closed, either with a basic edge or decorative flap. Repeat with the remaining fabric. Enjoy your clothes while deterring moths.

STEP FOUR Remember to replace the lavender if the fragrance fades so you have year-round protection from new moth eggs. If you can't smell the lavender anymore, neither can they!

243
PROTECT FABRICS WITH CEDAR

Red cedar has been used for many generations to ward off moths. If lavender is too floral for your tastes, cedar is a great alternative. Some entire closets and clothes-storing chests are lined or built from cedar, but you can also find them as small balls or as hanging blocks. As with lavender, it's the scent of cedar that deters moths, so it's important to renew the scent when it wanes. A light sanding will do the trick, plus a coat of cedar oil, sold in many home-supply stores.

244
CHASE THE MOTHS

It takes only one noticeable moth hole in a favorite skirt to make moth prevention a priority. The moths themselves don't harm fabrics; it's their larvae that feed on natural fibers like wool, silk, and feathers. Every spring—before you put winter clothes and wool blankets away—follow these easy steps to protect against moth holes.

CLEAN You can get rid of any hard-to-see larvae or eggs by doing a full cleaning of your closet (see item 241), including those hard-to-reach shelves and any boxes of shoes that you have seldom worn.

LAUNDER Dry-clean or wash all winter clothes before storing them. It's often dirty clothes with perspiration, perfume scents, and food stains that attract moths in the first place.

PROTECT Store clothing in airtight plastic boxes or bags over the summer. Use packing tape to seal the lids, and block even the tiniest airspace where a moth could possibly enter and lay eggs.

245
DESTROY DUST MITES

Dust mites are rarely a big issue if you regularly wash your sheets and clean your bedroom. But to be on the safe side, make sure you're doing the following to chase the mites away.

HEAT Wash bed sheets, mattress covers, pillows, and pillow covers in water heated to at least 130 degrees Fahrenheit (54 degrees Celsius), and dry on high heat.

REPLACE Buy new comforters and pillows every two years.

PROTECT Use allergenic, dust mite–averse pillow and mattress covers. Plastic is the best to prevent mites.

FILTER Vacuum often, and be sure your vacuum has a high-efficiency particulate air (HEPA) filter.

DRY Maintain low humidity levels in the house—dust mites thrive in humidity.

RESTRAIN Keep pets out of the bedroom. Dust mites love pet dander.

CHILL Set the thermostat at 70 degrees Fahrenheit or less.

246
ELIMINATE LICE

It's not the end of the world if you get word that your child has lice. It's a common rite of passage, so don't panic, but do act quickly and efficiently. Ask your pediatrician for expert recommendations on how to eliminate lice on the head, then focus on these steps to prevent them from infesting the house.

STEP ONE Identify everything that may have come in contact with the head—bedding, stuffed animals, hairbrush, comb, hats, headsets, coats, clothes.

STEP TWO Wash all the bedding and clothing in the washing machine at high heat for an extended cycle, even if it requires multiple loads. Soak hair brushes and hair accessories for an hour in water heated to at least 130 degrees Fahrenheit (54 degrees Celsius). Gather nonwashables—such as headphones and delicate hats—seal in a plastic bag, and put the bag in the freezer for 24 hours.

STEP THREE For pieces too large to go in the washer or freezer, put them in an airtight plastic bag and leave it sealed for 2 weeks to suffocate the lice.

STEP FOUR Vacuum all surfaces, including mattresses, rugs, and carpets.

STEP FIVE Check everyone's head every day until the lice are gone, following your doctor's orders, and once a week for a month afterward to make sure no more eggs have hatched.

BEDROOM
Checklists

Start your day off on the right foot by implementing a cleaning routine to give your bedroom the care it deserves. It only takes a few minutes each morning and night to check off your list. If you maintain a certain level of order and cleanliness, you'll have more time to enjoy the things that matter most. A little effort each day enables you to enjoy a relaxing evening and wake up to a stress-free morning.

Numbers refer to the general cleaning entries, so make sure to reference the appropriate supporting items to address specific materials and circumstances.

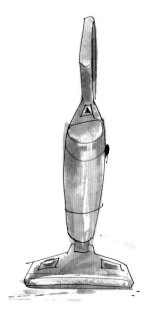

DAILY

- ☐ Spot-clean spills and potential stains
- ☐ Sweep or vacuum floors *30*
- ☐ Put dirty clothes in hamper *105*
- ☐ Make beds *234*
- ☐ Declutter dresser and nightstand *236*
- ☐ _____

WEEKLY

- ☐ Dust window treatments *14*
- ☐ Dust doors and baseboards *18*
- ☐ Clean switch plates *19*
- ☐ Dust ceilings and walls *20*
- ☐ Vacuum carpets and area rugs *42, 44*
- ☐ Dust lamps and lampshades *51*
- ☐ Wipe wooden furniture *179*
- ☐ Wash bed linens *220*
- ☐ Disinfect humidifier *239*
- ☐ Dust under furniture *240*
- ☐ _____
- ☐ _____
- ☐ _____

MONTHLY

- ☐ Clean mirrors *13*
- ☐ Clean window treatments *14*
- ☐ Wash trash bins *28*
- ☐ Clean doorknobs *29*
- ☐ Polish wood furniture *178*
- ☐ Wash pillow covers *222*
- ☐ Wash comforter cover *228*
- ☐ Vacuum mattress *230*
- ☐ Wash mattress pad *231*
- ☐ Dust bed frame *235*
- ☐ _____
- ☐ _____

SEASONALLY (SPRING AND FALL)

- ☐ Wash windows *12*
- ☐ Deep-clean window treatments *14*
- ☐ Wipe doors and baseboards *18*
- ☐ Deep-clean ceilings and walls *20*
- ☐ Deep-clean lampshades *53*
- ☐ Clean lamp bases and sconces *54, 55*
- ☐ Clean ceiling fixtures *57*
- ☐ Wash pillows and comforters *226, 229*
- ☐ Clean mattress *230*
- ☐ Treat bed curtains and skirts *232*
- ☐ Clean dresser drawers *236*
- ☐ Clean ceiling fan *237*
- ☐ Clean closet *241*
- ☐ Clean and store winter clothing *244*
- ☐ _____

called *yesterday* and the other is
called *tomorrow*, so today is
the right day to love, believe,
do and mostly live."

34.

247
CLEAN A COMPUTER

It's inevitable that a computer will begin to show a smudged screen, dirty keyboard, and dusty vents. Not only is that uninviting to work on, but accumulated dust can interfere with performance. Always check the owner's manual for specific care requirements before cleaning. It takes only a few minutes once a week to keep your computer looking new.

As with all electronics, remember that even a stray drop of water can prove fatal, so keep cleaning fluids at a safe distance to avoid spills, and make sure that all cleaning cloths are only slightly damp—always tightly squeeze as much moisture as possible out of the cleaning cloth to avoid drips or accumulated moisture. And let your electronics sit unused for a few hours after cleaning to make sure even trace amounts of moisture have dried up.

SCREEN A dry microfiber cloth will pick up any dust on the screen. Put the least amount of water possible in a corner of the cloth to wipe away fingerprints or smudges, but be careful not to put any pressure on the screen itself.

KEYBOARD Spray compressed air in bursts to blow away dust hiding in crevices—you may want to unplug the keyboard and do this outside if you expect a lot of debris. If you haven't used a can of compressed air before, practice and use the can's extension wand, which will help your precision. Be wary of holding the can too close to the keyboard, as it will produce condensation that's harmful to the keyboard's electronics.

After loosening any dust with the compressed air, turn the board upside down and gently shake it to dislodge debris. For dirt and grime on the keys or board frame, wipe with a cloth just moistened with an alcohol solution of one part rubbing alcohol to one part water. Dip a cotton swab in the alcohol solution and clean between each key. Wipe again with a dry cloth.

MOUSE Unplug the mouse from your computer and remove any batteries. Clean the mouse's exterior with a barely damp microfiber cloth and dry with a second cloth. Don't remove the scroll wheel; instead, turn the mouse upside down and roll the wheel to spin out dust.

For an optical mouse, very gently wipe the lens with a cotton swab dampened with the alcohol solution. Use a cloth dampened with a solution of one part alcohol to one part water to clean the rubber feet on the bottom to ensure that the mouse glides easily.

To clean a mouse with a rolling ball, turn it over and remove the bottom panel to release the ball. Clean the ball with a microfiber cloth dampened with a solution of one part alcohol to one part water, let it dry, then put the mouse back together. Refer to the owner's manual for any other internal cleaning instructions.

CASE Turn the computer off and unplug it. Wipe the exterior desktop case or laptop casing with a microfiber cloth slightly dampened with mild, soapy water. A cotton swab dipped in the soapy water cleans vents and tight corners. Repeat, wiping the outside again with a clean, damp cloth to remove any remaining soap, and then dry with a clean cloth.

CORDS Anything I can do to keep the room air dust-free helps my computer, so I wipe the entire cord and plug with a microfiber cloth, too.

ACCESSORIES Items such as a mouse pad, keyboard pad, or desk blotter can also accumulate dust or grime, especially from the oils in your skin. Give them a thorough wipedown with the All-Purpose Cleaner (see item 197) and let them dry fully before putting back into place.

248
DECLUTTER THE DESK

Flat surfaces can be hazardous; it's too easy to pile papers on top, thinking you'll deal with them later. The desk is likely to be the largest surface in the office and, as such, catches all.

REMOVE Take everything off your desk and out of the drawers. Stash papers in one basket and miscellaneous items in another to sort through after you clean the desk.

CLEAN Wipe down the entire desk, including the legs and inside the drawers, and every bin, pencil tray, stapler, and so on, using the Nonabrasive Vinegar Cleaner (see item 197).

SORT Once the desk is clean, sort through the two baskets of papers and miscellaneous items. File, shred, or recycle all the papers, and toss office supplies you no longer need.

249
GET ORGANIZED

A home office is a much-needed space to pay bills, organize tax-related documents, keep up with the school calendar, and perhaps do homework. But it has to be clean and orderly for us to work efficiently. You know by now that I'm a big advocate of removing clutter from your living environment, but nowhere is it more important than in a home office. A messy workspace prevents you from getting your tasks done.

In my first book, *The Complete Book of Home Organizing*, I included valuable advice for controlling the mail, school information, and tax and home records that drift through your life and office. Address the clutter, and then cleaning your office space will be easy, helping you maintain the ideal work-life balance.

252
REFRESH AN OFFICE CHAIR

Vacuum fabric with a dust-brush attachment, and use a microfiber cloth to pick up dust on leather and vinyl upholstery. If needed, try a gentle soap-and-water solution on a stain after testing on an inconspicuous spot. Spray casters with the All-Purpose Cleaner (see item 197). Wipe with a microfiber cloth, and use a cotton swab dampened with the All-Purpose Cleaner to get tight spots.

250
OPTIMIZE SHELF SPACE

Take everything off the office shelves and set aside. Spray the All-Purpose Cleaner (see item 197) lightly on the shelves and wipe clean with a microfiber cloth. Clean each shelf top to bottom, side to side. Clear out anything that has fallen behind the shelves or cabinet. If you have adjustable shelves, rethink their configuration to maximize the space. The height between shelves should accommodate a collection of similarly sized books, with the largest, heaviest or most often-used on the bottom shelf.

253
GO PAPERLESS

Instead of putting papers back into a filing cabinet, consider scanning nonessential documents and electronically storing them on your computer. Scanning is quick and painless, and you can always print them if you need a physical copy. Name the scan appropriately and drag it into an electronic folder, then recycle the paper, but make sure to shred anything with your Social Security number or any confidential information. Get in the habit of scanning as soon as you've dealt with a bill, letter, or valuable document, and the dreaded stack of papers to be filed will be a thing of the past!

251
CLEAN OUT THE FILING CABINET

Dust, crumbs, and paper clips frequently fall through to the bottom of a filing cabinet, so plan on cleaning it twice a year.

EMPTY Remove all the files and folders so that the drawers are empty; transfer them to a cardboard filing box to keep them organized.

VACUUM Use the dust-brush attachment to vacuum the drawers and get rid of all the built-up debris.

WIPE Spray the All-Purpose Cleaner (see item 197) on a microfiber cloth and wipe the outside of the cabinet.

RENEW Remove the drawers and vacuum underneath, as well as the rails. Replace the drawers, but as you put everything back, go through your files and sort, archive, shred, and recycle.

Quick Tip

TUNE UP STICKY DRAWERS

If desk drawers are sticking, take them out and turn them upside down so you can see the runners on the bottom of the drawer. Slide a wax candle or bar of soap along all the runners and the back of the drawer, transferring the lubricating wax, which will help prevent sticking.

On the spines of the binders: ABFOL DOCUMENTS · RECEIPTS · REPORTS · BUDGET · TAXES & PAYROLL

254
KEEP IT CURRENT

Whether used as an inspiration board or command central for recording save-the-dates and other events, a messy bulletin board layered with outdated information just gets ignored. Check it weekly and toss invitations and notices that are no longer relevant, and organize what remains for eye-catching impact. Dust the cork with a barely damp microfiber cloth and wipe down the sides and back of the board.

255
DISCARD OR DONATE

Be sure books, binders, and reference materials on your shelves are still useful, relevant, and easy to find. Don't keep materials that you only need once a year close at hand.

BOOKS If a book is no longer pertinent, donate it. How-to books on electronics, for example, are quickly dated after a few years. Better yet, trade in your hardbacks for e-books and save yourself from cleaning the bookshelf altogether.

BINDERS Once a project or remodeling effort is finished, the schedules, receipts, and addresses you saved no longer need to be readily accessible, so file them away or consider scanning them and recycling the paper.

REFERENCE After you file taxes, that year's records should be put away with a copy of the tax return.

While you're dusting each book or binder, think about the layout of the newly arranged bookshelf. Don't squeeze books in so they're too tight to pull out or prop them, stressing the binding. Arrange them so the most used are the most readily available.

OFFICE
Checklists

Whether you're in the office every day or just evenings when you take care of household bills and chores, the office should be organized and stress-free. Plan your cleaning activities so they become a ritual, part of the day-to-day process that brings out the best in you!

Numbers refer to the general cleaning entries, so make sure to reference the appropriate supporting items to address specific materials and circumstances.

DAILY

- ☐ Spot-clean spills and potential stains
- ☐ Sweep or vacuum floors *30*
- ☐ Declutter desktop *248*
- ☐ Sort through mail *248*
- ☐ _____
- ☐ _____
- ☐ _____

WEEKLY

- ☐ Dust window treatments *14*
- ☐ Dust doors and baseboards *18*
- ☐ Clean switch plates *19*
- ☐ Dust ceilings and walls *20*
- ☐ Vacuum carpets and area rugs *42, 44*
- ☐ Dust lamp shades and chandeliers *52, 56*
- ☐ Dust surfaces and accessories *170*
- ☐ Wipe wooden furniture *179*
- ☐ Clean computer *247*
- ☐ Wipe and declutter desk *248*
- ☐ Clear bulletin board *254*
- ☐ Empty trash can
- ☐ _____

MONTHLY

- ☐ Clean mirrors *13*
- ☐ Clean window treatments *14*
- ☐ Wash trash bins *28*
- ☐ Clean doorknobs *29*
- ☐ Polish wood furniture *178*
- ☐ Dust books and bookshelves *194, 195*
- ☐ Vacuum office chair *252*

SEASONALLY (SPRING AND FALL)

- ☐ Wash windows *12*
- ☐ Deep-clean window treatments *14*
- ☐ Wipe doors and baseboards *18*
- ☐ Clean walls *20*
- ☐ Clean exterior doors *27*
- ☐ Deep-clean lampshades *53*
- ☐ Clean lamp bases and sconces *54, 55*
- ☐ Clean fixtures *57*
- ☐ Deep-clean desk *248*
- ☐ Deep-clean shelves *250*
- ☐ Clean filing cabinet *254*
- ☐ _____
- ☐ _____
- ☐ _____
- ☐ _____
- ☐ _____
- ☐ _____
- ☐ _____
- ☐ _____

Cleaning Checklists

30-BAG PURGE
Challenge

One of the biggest obstacles I hear from readers is how to deal with the amount of clutter everyone has accumulated over the years. It's a challenge to get organized and on a regular cleaning schedule when you have mountains of clutter to compete with. So before you begin cleaning and organizing, clear the chaos from your home. The purge is designed for you to go at your own pace. You can purge it all in one day, designate weekends only, or purge one bag per day. Customize it to fit your needs.

DAY 1	DAY 2	DAY 3	DAY 4	DAY 5	DAY 6
Shoes	Magazines & Newspapers	Food Storage Containers	Empty Bottles & Cleaners	Paper Piles	Toiletries & Make up
DAY 7	**DAY 8**	**DAY 9**	**DAY 10**	**DAY 11**	**DAY 12**
Nightstand	Refrigerator	Junk Drawer	Master Closet	Car	Handbag
DAY 13	**DAY 14**	**DAY 15**	**DAY 16**	**DAY 17**	**DAY 18**
Dresser Drawers	Books	DVDs & CDs	Linen Closet	Holiday Décor	Toys & Hobbies
DAY 19	**DAY 20**	**DAY 21**	**DAY 22**	**DAY 23**	**DAY 24**
Pantry	Kids Clothing	Kitchen Cabinets	Winterwear	Bags & Luggage	Laundry Room
DAY 25	**DAY 26**	**DAY 27**	**DAY 28**	**DAY 29**	**DAY 30**
Garage or Utility Closet	Games & Puzzles	Accessories	Home Décor	Small Appliances	Fill a Bag

DAILY

Checklists

Use this master checklist of daily cleaning suggestions to create a routine that works for you. You can customize the list to create a cleaning system that works for your home and your schedule. You'll be amazed at the difference you can make by investing just a few extra minutes each morning and evening!

Kitchen

- ☐ Sweep or vacuum floors *30*
- ☐ Wipe counters and tables *89*
- ☐ Wipe stovetop *68*
- ☐ Wash dishes *73*
- ☐ Load and run dishwasher *77*
- ☐ Wipe dishwasher exterior *76*
- ☐ Clean sink *82*
- ☐ Wipe faucets *86*
- ☐ Clean minor appliances *92*
- ☐ Put out new dishtowels *59*

Bathroom

- ☐ Sweep or vacuum floors *30*
- ☐ Put dirty clothes in hamper *105*
- ☐ Wipe faucets *105*
- ☐ Wipe sinks and counters *105*
- ☐ Squeegee shower *105*
- ☐ Rinse bathtub *105*
- ☐ Rinse and dry whirlpool *105*
- ☐ Swish toilets *138*

Laundry Room

- ☐ Sweep or vacuum floors *30*
- ☐ Declutter laundry room *150*

- ☐ Spot-treat stains *156*
- ☐ Wash clothes *150*
- ☐ Dry clothes *165*
- ☐ Clean lint filter *166*

Living Room

- ☐ Quick pick-up *169*
- ☐ Spot-clean spills and potential stains
- ☐ Straighten throw pillows
- ☐ Sweep or vacuum floors *30*

Dining Room

- ☐ Spot-clean spills and potential stains
- ☐ Sweep or vacuum floors *30*
- ☐ Spot-clean table linens *156*

- ☐ Wash table linens *201*
- ☐ Clear table of clutter *198*
- ☐ Wipe dining room table *213*

Bedroom

- ☐ Spot-clean spills and potential stains
- ☐ Sweep or vacuum floors *30*
- ☐ Put dirty clothes in hamper *105*
- ☐ Make beds *234*
- ☐ Declutter dresser and nightstand *236*

Office

- ☐ Spot-clean spills and potential stains
- ☐ Sweep or vacuum floors *30*
- ☐ Declutter desktop *248*
- ☐ Sort through mail *248*

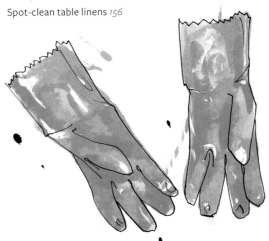

WEEKLY

Checklists

Set aside a few hours each weekend to keep your home looking great! If you prefer to reserve weekends for family and friends, designate some time during the weekdays to accomplish these tasks. That way you'll have the satisfaction that comes with a job well done as you relax and recharge. You've earned it!

Kitchen

- ☐ Dust window treatments *14*
- ☐ Dust doors and baseboards *18*
- ☐ Clean switch plates *19*
- ☐ Dust ceilings and walls *20*
- ☐ Mop floors *31*
- ☐ Dust lampshades and chandeliers *52, 56*
- ☐ Clean refrigerator interior/ exterior *61*
- ☐ Clean stovetop *68*
- ☐ Clean disposal *83*
- ☐ Wipe cabinet doors *100*
- ☐ Disinfect handles and knobs *103*

Bathroom

- ☐ Clean mirrors *13*
- ☐ Dust window treatments *14*
- ☐ Dust doors and baseboards *18*
- ☐ Clean switch plates *19*
- ☐ Dust ceilings and walls *20*
- ☐ Mop floors *31*
- ☐ Freshen air *107*
- ☐ Scrub shower *111*
- ☐ Deep-clean tub *115*

- ☐ Wash towels, bathmats, and bathrobes *119*
- ☐ Clean sink *122*
- ☐ Wash makeup and hair brushes *134*
- ☐ Wash canisters, glasses, soap dishes *136*
- ☐ Wipe down toilet exterior and tank *138*
- ☐ Clean bidet *140*
- ☐ Clean toilet brush *141*

Laundry Room

- ☐ Dust window treatments *14*
- ☐ Dust doors and baseboards *18*
- ☐ Clean switch plates *19*
- ☐ Dust ceilings and walls *20*
- ☐ Mop floors *31*
- ☐ Wipe down washer and dryer

Living Room

- ☐ Dust window treatments *14*
- ☐ Dust doors and baseboards *18*
- ☐ Clean switch plates *19*

- ☐ Dust ceilings and walls *20*
- ☐ Vacuum carpets and area rugs *42, 44*
- ☐ Dust lampshades and chandeliers *52, 56*
- ☐ Dust surfaces and accessories *170*
- ☐ Wipe wooden furniture *179*
- ☐ Dust television *191*
- ☐ Clean remote controls *193*

Dining Room

- ☐ Dust window treatments *14*
- ☐ Dust doors and baseboards *18*
- ☐ Clean switch plates *19*
- ☐ Dust ceilings and walls *20*
- ☐ Mop floors *31*
- ☐ Vacuum carpets and area rugs *42, 44*
- ☐ Dust sconces and chandeliers *52, 56*
- ☐ Dust sconces, lampshades, and chandeliers *52, 54, 56*

Bedroom

Office

MONTHLY

Checklists

The whole house needs a thorough cleaning once a month to freshen it up from everyday wear. Use this list to help stay on top of the infrequent and deep-cleaning tasks that require your attention.

Kitchen

- ☐ Clean window treatments *14*
- ☐ Wash trash bins *28*
- ☐ Clean doorknobs *29*
- ☐ Steam-clean microwave *67*
- ☐ Sanitize dishwasher interior *78*
- ☐ Deep-clean disposal *83*
- ☐ Deep-clean minor appliances *92*
- ☐ Clean knobs *103*

Bathroom

- ☐ Clean window treatments *14*
- ☐ Wash trash bins *28*
- ☐ Sanitize whirlpool tub *117*
- ☐ Clear drains *118*
- ☐ Clean tub exterior *116*
- ☐ Deep-clean toilet bowl and tank *138*
- ☐ Remove minerals from toilet *139*

Laundry Room

- ☐ Clean window treatments *14*
- ☐ Wash trash bins *28*
- ☐ Clean doorknobs *29*
- ☐ Clean washer *160*
- ☐ Clean sink *122*
- ☐ Sweep and mop behind washer and dryer

Living Room

- ☐ Clean mirrors *13*
- ☐ Clean window treatments *14*
- ☐ Wash trash bins *28*
- ☐ Clean doorknobs *29*
- ☐ Vacuum upholstered furniture *171, 176*
- ☐ Clean leather upholstery *176*
- ☐ Polish wood furniture *179*
- ☐ Dust and clean speakers *192*
- ☐ Dust books and bookshelves *194, 195*

Dining Room

- ☐ Clean mirrors *13*
- ☐ Clean window treatments *14*
- ☐ Clean doorknobs *29*
- ☐ Clean sconces, chandeliers, and light fixtures *54, 56, 57*
- ☐ Polish wooden furniture *214*

Bedroom

- ☐ Clean mirrors *13*
- ☐ Clean window treatments *14*
- ☐ Wash trash bins *28*
- ☐ Clean doorknobs *29*
- ☐ Polish wooden furniture *178*
- ☐ Wash pillow covers *222*
- ☐ Wash comforter cover *228*
- ☐ Vacuum mattress *230*
- ☐ Wash mattress pad *231*
- ☐ Dust bed frame *235*

Office

- ☐ Clean mirrors *13*
- ☐ Clean window treatments *14*
- ☐ Wash trash bins *28*
- ☐ Clean doorknobs *29*
- ☐ Dust Window treatments *14*
- ☐ Polish wooden furniture *178*
- ☐ Dust books and bookshelves *194, 195*
- ☐ Vacuum office chair *252*

SEASONAL Checklists

Every spring and fall, plan for a thorough seasonal cleaning that prepares your household for the next six months. Tackle these big events as a whole family and everyone will feel the satisfaction of a team effort. If you want to make seasonal cleaning feel less like a chore and more like a game, take a look at Nikki's Spring Cleaning Box in the Getting Started section!

Kitchen

- ☐ Wash windows *12*
- ☐ Deep-clean window treatments *14*
- ☐ Wipe doors and baseboards *18*
- ☐ Clean walls *20*
- ☐ Clean light fixtures, chandeliers, and sconces *54, 56, 57*
- ☐ Deep-clean refrigerator and freezer *61*
- ☐ Replace liners *61*
- ☐ Clean condenser coils *63*
- ☐ Deep-clean stove and oven *66*
- ☐ Clean vent hood and filter *72*
- ☐ Deep-clean dishwasher and filter *79*
- ☐ Scour disposal *83*
- ☐ Clean knife block *93*
- ☐ Clean out cabinets and pantry *99*
- ☐ Clean inside cabinets and drawers *99*
- ☐ Reseal countertops *89*

Bathroom

- ☐ Wash windows *12*
- ☐ Deep-clean window treatments *14*
- ☐ Wipe doors and baseboards *18*
- ☐ Clean walls *20*
- ☐ Clean sconces and light fixtures *54, 57*
- ☐ Remove clutter *110*
- ☐ Purge medicine cabinet *108*
- ☐ Wash shower curtain *111*
- ☐ Clean showerhead *112*
- ☐ Clean vent *113*
- ☐ Clean grout *114*
- ☐ Clean shelves, drawers, and cabinets *125*
- ☐ Clean makeup drawer *126*
- ☐ Clean jewelry box *127*
- ☐ Restock bathroom caddy *106*

Laundry Room

- ☐ Wash windows *12*
- ☐ Deep-clean window treatments *14*
- ☐ Wipe doors and baseboards *18*
- ☐ Clean walls *20*
- ☐ Clean sconces and light fixtures *54, 57*
- ☐ Clean iron *153*
- ☐ Clean washer *162, 163*
- ☐ Clean dryer vent *166*
- ☐ Restock cleaning caddy *1*
- ☐ Restock laundry supplies *155, 157*

Living Room

- ☐ Wash windows *12*
- ☐ Deep-clean window treatments *14*
- ☐ Wipe doors and baseboards *18*
- ☐ Clean walls *20*
- ☐ Clean exterior doors *27*
- ☐ Deep-clean lampshades *53*
- ☐ Clean lamp bases *55*
- ☐ Clean sconces, chandeliers, and light fixtures *54, 56, 57*
- ☐ Deep-clean upholstery *171*
- ☐ Deep-clean fireplace *181*
- ☐ Clean framed art *189*
- ☐ Clean and vacuum bookshelves *195*
- ☐ Dust plants *196*
- ☐ Hire a chimney sweep *184*

Dining Room

- ☐ Wash windows *12*
- ☐ Deep-clean window treatments *14*
- ☐ Wipe doors and baseboards *18*
- ☐ Clean walls *20*
- ☐ Deep-clean lampshades *53*
- ☐ Clean lamp bases and sconces *54, 55*

Office

Bedroom

Recipes

All the recipes in the chapters throughout this book can be found here for easy reference. Making your own natural cleaning products will not just help the environment, but save you money that can be better spent on other things.

Basic Cleaners

ALL-PURPOSE CLEANER

2 tsp. borax, ¼ tsp. liquid castile soap, 10 drops lemon essential oil.

Mix all ingredients with hot water in a 16-oz. spray bottle.

DISINFECTANT

2 Tbsp. liquid castile soap, 20 drops tea tree oil.

Mix the soap and essential oil with hot water in a 16-oz. spray bottle.

GLASS CLEANER

¼ c. distilled white vinegar, 5 drops lemon essential oil.

Mix all ingredients with hot water in a 16-oz. spray bottle.

NONABRASIVE VINEGAR CLEANER

1 part distilled white vinegar, 2 parts water, 5 drops lavender essential oil.

Combine the vinegar and water in a 16-oz. spray bottle. Add 5 drops of essential oils if you don't like the smell of vinegar—my favorites are lavender, grapefruit, orange, lemon, and peppermint.

Bathroom Cleaners

DRAIN CLEANER

1 c. table salt, 1 c. baking soda, 1 c. distilled vinegar

Thoroughly mix the salt and baking soda in a small bowl. Boil 2–3 qt. water in a kettle. Pour the salt and baking soda mixture down the drain, and slowly pour the vinegar into the drain. Let it bubble for 1–2 minutes. Clear the drain by pouring in the boiling water. Wipe the drain cover with a soft cloth to make sure no salt or vinegar remains.

GROUT CLEANER

¾ c. baking soda, ½ c. hydrogen peroxide, 2–3 c. water

Mix all ingredients into a paste, apply, and let sit for 15 minutes. Scrub with a grout brush or toothbrush, staying within the grout lines.

TOILET BOWL BOMBS

1½ c. baking soda, ½ c. citric acid powder, 20 drops peppermint essential oil

Thoroughly mix the baking soda and citric acid powder in a bowl. Slowly stir in the peppermint essential oil to evenly distribute. Use a spray bottle

to sparingly mist water to the mixture—stirring to uniformly moisten the powder—until the powder will stick together in clumps. The mixture will slightly fizz from the moisture, so make sure not to oversaturate.

Firmly pack a silicone mold with the moist mixture and leave out to dry overnight, wiping off any excess from the fizzing. Gently remove the formed bombs from the mold and store in a sealable container.

Add a finished bomb to the toilet bowl and allow to fizz. Once the bomb has dissolved, flush out the bowl water.

TOILET BOWL CLEANER

Liquid castile soap, baking soda

Squirt the liquid castile soap under the rim of the toilet bowl, then sprinkle ½ c. baking soda into the bowl. Scrub with a toilet brush, and flush to rinse.

TUB 'N' TILE CLEANER

½ c. borax, ½ c. baking soda, 1 tsp. liquid castile soap

Thoroughly mix all ingredients in a bucket with 2–3 c. hot water.

Carpet and Furniture Cleaners

BASIC CARPET STAIN REMOVER

¼ tsp. castile soap

Mix in a 16-oz. spray bottle.

VINEGAR-BASED CARPET STAIN REMOVER

1 Tbsp. castile soap, 1 Tbsp. white vinegar, 2 c. warm water

Mix in a 16-oz. spray bottle.

FURNITURE POLISH

½ c. jojoba oil, 2 Tbsp. distilled white vinegar, 5 drops lemon essential oil

Pour the jojoba oil, vinegar, and essential oil in a sealable 8-oz. jar. Vigorously shake to emulsify before using.

Floor Cleaners

ALL-PURPOSE FLOOR CLEANER

1 tsp. almond castile soap, ¼ c. distilled white vinegar, 10 drops orange essential oil, 10 drops clove essential oil.

Mix all ingredients with hot water in a 24-oz. spray bottle.

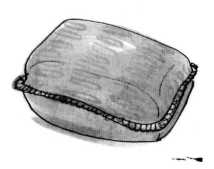

HARDWOOD FLOOR CLEANER

1 tsp. almond castile soap and 10 drops lemon essential oil.

Mix in a 24-oz. spray bottle with hot water. Use sparingly to minimize the chance of warping; do not use on unsealed hardwoods.

LAMINATE FLOOR CLEANER

¾ c. distilled white vinegar, ¾ c. rubbing alcohol, 10 drops peppermint essential oil.

Mix in a 24-oz. spray bottle with ¾ c. hot water. Use sparingly to minimize the chance of warping.

TILE FLOOR CLEANER

¼ c. distilled white vinegar and 15 drops orange essential oil.

Mix in a 24-oz. spray bottle with hot water.

VINYL FLOOR CLEANER

¼ c. distilled white vinegar, 3 Tbsp. borax, 10 drops of lemon and 10 drops of lavender essential oil.

Mix in a 24-oz. spray bottle with hot water.

Kitchen Cleaners

GARBAGE DISPOSAL BOMBS

(makes 24 bombs) ½ c. citric acid, 1½ c. baking soda, 30 drops orange essential oil.

Mix all ingredients in a bowl until thoroughly combined. Use a spray bottle to mist just enough water for the mixture to hold its shape. Mold the mixture into small balls with a rounded tablespoon and place on a cookie sheet to dry overnight. Store in an airtight container.

Laundry Products

BLEACHING SOLUTION

1 c. hydrogen peroxide, ¼ c. lemon juice, 3 qt. water

Thoroughly mix in a large container. Pour 1–2 c. per wash load into the bleach dispenser.

POWDERED LAUNDRY DETERGENT

3 bars of Dr. Bronner's or Fels Naphtha soap (shredded), 1 (4 lb.) box of borax, 1 (4 lb.) box of super washing soda, 1 (4 lb.) box of baking soda

Shred the soap in a food processor or with a cheese grater. Mix all ingredients in a large, sealable container.

Directions: Use 2 heaping tablespoons in a top-load machine, less for an HE washer.

Index

C

Index

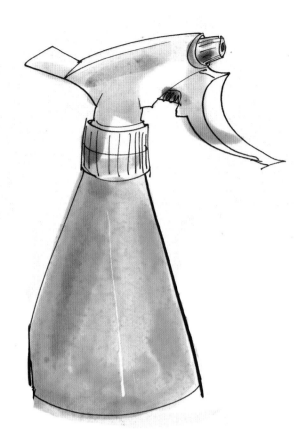

G

H

Index

Index

Acknowledgments

I am so thankful to be able to write a sister book to *The Complete Book of Home Organization*, rounding out the home-keeping process. God has truly blessed me and given me an ideal platform to inspire others. If I've helped just one person improve their quality of life by implementing a cleaning routine that allows them to get their life back on track, I feel that I've succeeded.

Many thanks to Weldon Owen for giving me another go around and allowing me to share encouragement to others who struggle. To my editor Kevin Toyama, your expertise and ability to fill in the blanks is a talent that I deeply admire. To Katherine Pearson and Francie MacDougal, thank you for being the guiding force of this book. To my designer, Jennifer Durant—who has more patience than anyone I've ever known—I'm profoundly grateful. To Publisher Roger Shaw, Associate Publisher Mariah Bear, Creative Director Kelly Booth, Art Director Allister Fein, Associate Editor Ian Cannon, Associate Production Director Michelle Duggan, Senior Publicity Manager Jamie Antoniou, Associate Marketing Manager Cathy Hebert, Copyeditor Mark Nichol, Indexer Kevin Broccoli, Illustration Coordinator Conor Buckley, Illustrator Louise Morgan, and Illustrator Juan Calle, thank you for creating another fabulous book. To Nikki Boyd, thank you for sharing your talents once again.

I can't sign off without thanking my fans, my online community, and the many friends from around the world. Without you, this book would not be in the hands of so many. You are my encouragement, my inspiration, and my "why."

Finally, I am so blessed to have such a wonderful family and support system with whom to share my successes. To Alex, Gavin, and Abigail: I'm deeply proud of each one of you. You are the reasons I strive for more. And to my husband and soul mate John, thank you for being the support that I need on a daily basis. I cannot imagine doing life without you. I love all of you with my whole heart.

About the Author

Toni Hammersley is the creator of www.abowlfulloflemons.net, a home-keeping website that encourages thousands around the world to get their lives in order. She's the author of the inspiring and wildly popular book *The Complete Book of Home Organization*, and hosts yearly challenges that help her community of readers purge their clutter and get organized. She lives in Charleston, South Carolina, with her husband and three children.

Credits

All photos copyright of Toni Hammersley except as follows: Africa Studio/shutterstock: 079; Akira3288/shutterstock: 042; Jean Allsopp Photography/Paige Schnell at Tracery Interiors: Cover photo, Kitchen opener, 072, full spread before Kitchen Checklist, full spread after Recipes; baloon/shutterstock: 077; Tracey Ayton: Laundry opener; Lincoln Barbour: Title Page, 058, 066, full spread after Office Checklist; Amy Bartlam/Click Creative Inc.: Living Spaces opener; Breadmaker/shutterstock: 033; brizmaker/shutterstock: 069; Bunker Workshop (Interior)/Matt Delphenich (Photography): 098; Sara K Byrne Photography/Stocksy: 057 (Quick Tip); Beth Dana Design/Gazston Gal Photography: 027, 090, 091, 115, 122, 164; Elena Elisseeva/shutterstock: 012; Raymond Forbes/Stocksy: 127, 168, 182; Ryann Ford: 010, 082; marilook/shutterstock: 016; Interior Therapy (www.interiortherapy.co.uk): 138; Jodie Johnson/shutterstock: 121; Simon Kenny: 021; Kunertus/shutterstock: 075; Marta Locklear: 213; Lumina Images/Stocksy: 156; Kathryn MacDonald: 108, 111; Ray Main/Mainstream Images: Bathroom opener; papa studio/shutterstock: 176; Paul Matthew Photography/shutterstock: 030; Marian Parsons (missmustardseed.com): Bathroom intro, 150, 190, 207, 232, 236; One Three Design Inc./Stephani Buchman: Laundry intro; Aubrie Pick: TOC, Author intro, 008, 009, 032, 104, 149, 156 (spoons and jar of powder detergent), 157 197, 208, Cleaning Checklists opener, opposite Daily and Monthly Checklists (in Cleaning Checklists section), Recipe opener, imprint page, final grid of photos; Trinette Reed Photography/Stocksy: 105, 128, full spread after Bathroom Checklist; Kelly Scanlon Design/Onyx and Ash Studios (Photo): 056, 116; James Tarry/Stocksy: 142; Gillian van Niekerk/Stocksy: 200; Kristine Ridley Weilert/Stocksy: 185

Cover photo: Jean Allsopp (Photographer) &
Paige Schnell at Tracery Interiors (Interior Designer)

weldon**owen**

PRESIDENT & PUBLISHER	Roger Shaw
SVP, SALES & MARKETING	Amy Kaneko
FINANCE DIRECTOR	Philip Paulick
ASSOCIATE PUBLISHER	Mariah Bear
SENIOR EDITOR	Kevin Toyama
FREELANCE PROJECT EDITOR	Katherine Pearson
FREELANCE EDITOR	Francie MacDougall
ASSOCIATE EDITOR	Ian Cannon
CREATIVE DIRECTOR	Kelly Booth
ART DIRECTOR	Allister Fein
FREELANCE ART DIRECTOR	Jennifer Durrant
SENIOR PRODUCTION DESIGNER	Rachel Lopez Metzger
ILLUSTRATION COORDINATOR	Conor Buckley
PRODUCTION DIRECTOR	Chris Hemesath
ASSOCIATE PRODUCTION DIRECTOR	Michelle Duggan
IMAGING MANAGER	Don Hill

Weldon Owen would like to thank. Ethel Brennan, Aubrie Pick, and Miki Vargas for their beautiful photography and styling and Tammy White for her Photoshop skills and retouching. Mark Nichol for editorial expertise, and BIM Creatives for the index.

While every tip in this book has been fact-checked and tested, the publisher makes no warranty, express or implied, that the information is appropriate for every individual, situation, or purpose, and assumes no responsibility for errors or omissions. The information in this book is presented for informational value only. Always follow all manufacturer instructions for care and cleaning, and if a manufacturer does not recommend the materials or techniques presented herein, follow the manufacturer's recommendations. You assume the risk and full responsibility for all of your actions, and the publishers will not be held responsible for any loss or damage of any sort, whether consequential, incidental, special, or otherwise that may result from the information presented.